D1165214

# CUCKOO HILL

# CUCKOO HILL

## THE BOOK OF GORLEY

## HEYWOOD SUMNER

**J.M. Dent & Sons Ltd**
London and Melbourne

Designed and produced by
BELLEW PUBLISHING COMPANY LIMITED
7 Southampton Place, London WC1A 2DR

First published 1987

©L.J.C. Evans 1987
Introduction © Margot Coatts 1987

All rights reserved. No part of this publication
may be reproduced, stored in a retrieval system,
or transmitted, in any form or by any means,
electronic, mechanical, photocopying, recording
or otherwise, without the prior permission of
J.M. Dent & Sons Ltd

J.M. Dent & Sons Ltd
Aldine House, 33 Welbeck Street, London W1M 8LX

British Library Cataloguing in Publication Data
Sumner, Heywood.
[The Book of Gorley]. Cuckoo Hill:
the book of Gorley.
1. Natural history — England — New Forest
I. [The Book of Gorley]. II. Title
574.9422'75    QH138.N4

ISBN 0 460 04744 2

Origination by Brian Gregory Associates Ltd
Printed and bound in Spain by Graficromo, S.A.

*Endpapers*:
Wood-block printed wallpaper, 'Quercus', 1908.

# CONTENTS

# ACKNOWLEDGEMENTS

THE PUBLISHERS wish to thank the following for their help in the production of this book: Mr and Mrs L.J.C. Evans and members of the Evans and Heywood families for their generosity in allowing us to use the original manuscript; Margot Coatts for her enthusiasm and invaluable assistance; Miss Elizabeth Lewis, Curator of Winchester City Museum; Mrs Philippa Stevens, Local History Librarian of Hampshire County Library; Jude James, author and local historian; Mrs Susan Gibson and the late Charles Gibson; Bob Vickers; Steve West and Brian Gregory.

The publishers also wish to thank the following for permission to reproduce photographs: Elizabeth Lewis, page xi; Michael Walford of Short Publications, pages xvi, xvii, xxi; Winchester City Museums, pages viii, xii, xiii, xiv, xix, xxii-xxiii; Manchester City Art Galleries, endpapers.

# EDITOR'S NOTE

THIS BOOK is based on the original manuscript of *The Book of Gorley* by Heywood Sumner, which dates from 1904 to about 1909. During his life, Sumner added to the work in two further volumes at later dates but in the same style. An edited version of *The Book of Gorley* was published in a small edition by the Chiswick Press in 1910, for which the illustrations were redrawn as black and white line blocks.

The original manuscript contains a chapter on the local parish records which has been omitted in this book. Several gaps in the manuscript, which Sumner had left for illustrations but which remained unfilled, have also been removed. Consequently, in order to assist the reader, some sections of the book have been repaginated and certain illustrations transposed to a limited degree.

*The Book of Gorley* first came to the attention of Bellew Publishing through the splendid catalogue produced by the Winchester City Museum to accompany their exhibition on Sumner's life and work, shown in 1986.

# FOREWORD

———◇———

THIS BOOK is based on the earliest manuscript version of *The Book of Gorley*, which my great-uncle, Heywood Sumner, began in 1904. It has been a source of private enjoyment within the family ever since. During 1986, due largely to the inspiration and industry of Elizabeth Lewis and Margot Coatts and other Sumner admirers, successful exhibitions of his work were held in Winchester, Cheltenham and Portsmouth. The ensuing renewal of interest in Sumner's life and work suggested that *The Book of Gorley* might appeal to a wider circle of readers.

The book now published gives a picture of life on the edge of the New Forest at the beginning of this century; it describes how Heywood Sumner designed and built a house called Cuckoo Hill for himself and his family.

It is intended that royalties from the sale of the book shall go to a Heywood Sumner Trust, to be devoted to charitable purposes in the field of arts, crafts, archaeology and church decoration.

L.J.C. Evans
Shaftesbury,
January 1987

Heywood Sumner outside his studio at Cuckoo Hill, *c.* 1930.

# INTRODUCTION

H EYWOOD SUMNER was a major figure in the Arts and Crafts Movement in the 1880s and 1890s and a contemporary of such well-known figures as William Morris, C.R. Ashbee and Walter Crane. Yet in 1904 he turned his back on the artistic and commercial life of London and withdrew to Cuckoo Hill in the glorious countryside of the New Forest in Hampshire. Despite his first successful career as a book illustrator, designer of wallpapers and textiles, stained glass and sgraffito murals, he devoted the last thirty years of his life to the history of the Wessex countryside in which he had settled. He became a highly-respected self-taught field archaeologist and topographer. Sumner's works are among the most reliable sources of information on the region's topography, and he is regarded today by many local historians and professional archaeologists as one of the chief chroniclers of the New Forest and Cranborne Chase areas of southern England.

George Heywood Maunoir Sumner was born in Alresford, near Winchester, Hampshire, in 1853 into an influential family of Anglican clergy. His grandfather was Charles Henry Sumner, Bishop of Winchester; his father was George Henry Sumner, Rector of Alresford and later Suffragan Bishop of Guildford and his mother, Mary Sumner (née Heywood), founded the Mothers' Union. Sumner followed his father and grandfather to Eton and Christ Church, Oxford, where he read Classics then changed to Modern History. In 1876 he was admitted to Lincoln's Inn to read for the Bar; here he shared rooms with his childhood friend W.A.S. Benson, the designer. Heywood Sumner and his two sisters, Margaret Effie and Louisa Mary, had grown up with the Benson family in Alresford, and in 1883 Sumner married Agnes Benson.

By the time he was called to the Bar in 1879, Sumner was

already interested in art. A sketch book that he made as a young man is full of drawings of Germany and Switzerland, as well as of the area around Alresford. There is no doubt that, influenced by his Hampshire upbringing, Sumner regarded himself at the outset of his artistic career chiefly as a landscape artist. His first publication, a collection of etchings entitled *The Itchen Valley*, appeared when he was twenty-eight, and was well received by the public and critics alike. It was followed a year later by *The Avon: from Naseby to Tewkesbury*. He went on to make further studies for publications including *Epping Forest* by Edward North Buxton (1884) and *The New Forest* by John R. Wise (1883, 1888, and 1895), and continued to produce illustrated books all his life.

During the 1880s, and contemporary with his early landscape work, Heywood Sumner developed a striking and individual style for black and white illustration. Among his various designs for badges, headings and bookplates are those for the Arts and Crafts Exhibition Society and the Mothers' Union. In his designs for books of the same period, Sumner carefully integrated text, illustration, ornamental headings, tailpieces and cover design. His best-known examples are *The Besom Maker* (1888), a collection of English folk songs, and two books by De la Motte Fouqué: *Sintram and His Companions* (1883), a charming children's book, and *Undine* (1888). *Undine* anticipated the Art Nouveau and was the summit of his achievement in this field.

Throughout Sumner's career as an artist, whether in his church decorations, stained glass, book illustrations or wallpaper designs, traces of the techniques he was to employ and the interests he was to pursue in later years at Cuckoo Hill are visible. His sgraffito designs in the remote and tiny stone church of St Mary the Virgin at Llanfair Kilgeddin in South Wales are an example – like the Itchen and Avon etchings and *Cuckoo Hill* – of the way in which Sumner made use of a particular geographical location and produced an appreciation of it. The nineteen panels in the church skilfully depict the birds, beasts and fishes, the nearby Sugar Loaf Mountain and the River Usk; even the children who appear in the

'Blackdown Poplars', an etching from
*The Avon: From Naseby to Tewkesbury* (1882)

mural are said to come from the district. They are shown in
contemporary clothes, playing with hoop and stick.

His wallpapers, too, reflect his deep love of nature and are
among some of the most impressive of Sumner's colour work.
Produced over a period of about nineteen years, from 1893 to
1912, they are a manifestation of Sumner's fascination with the
shapes of plants: he loved the common columbine, rampant
bindweed or the untrained tree as much as the cultivated tulip,
vine, camellia, or peony. 'The Vine' (1893) is characteristic of

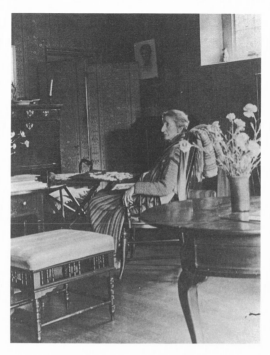

Agnes Sumner at Cuckoo Hill in front of
'Poole' wallpaper of 1906.

Sumner's early wallpaper designs, where plant forms were often arranged in tall panels; later designs show the plants arranged in box shapes (one of these designs, 'Poole', was used at Cuckoo Hill), and by 1908 the patterns were of a sober 'all-over' foliage in which a fine outline was a new characteristic ('Quercus', 1908; see endpapers).

Sumner's last grand decorative work, 'The Chace' tapestry, commissioned and woven by Morris & Co. in 1908, also reveals his detailed knowledge of the New Forest landscape. He set the design in a beech wood, possibly at Anses. The scene is a New Forest deer hunt in medieval times; the Forest floor is naturalistically exact and the geometric border pattern frames charming vignettes of foxes, rabbits and stoats. All the Forest woods, their trees and histories, were known to Sumner; the massive oaks and yews in Redshoot or Sloden woods illustrated in *Cuckoo Hill* are reminiscent of his work in Southeran's 'Artists Edition' of Wise's *The New Forest*.

It is not surprising that in 1897, when Sumner became dissatisfied with urban life and concerned for his wife Agnes's poor health, he decided to return to the country. The family moved first to Bournemouth, where they lived in a house called Skerryvore, once the home of Robert Louis Stevenson. During the time that they lived here Sumner was still heavily involved in a sgraffito scheme at the church of All Saints, Ennismore Gardens, London, as well as with exhibitions and stained glass commissions in Oxfordshire and Essex, but he managed to find the time to go for long bicycle rides in the New Forest. As Sumner writes in the first chapter of *Cuckoo Hill*, 'the country inland was a constant joy' and from the information that he gathered on these trips he 'got to know about the buying and selling of land round the Forest, and how hard it was to get a good site, and thus I began the dream of possession'. When, after several years in Bournemouth, Agnes's health showed no sign of improvement, Heywood Sumner followed his 'own inclinations' and bought some land at Cuckoo Hill, South Gorley, on the edge of the New Forest, on which to build a house.

Pencil, pen and ink and watercolour cartoon for 'The Chace' tapestry, *c.* 1908.

Sgraffito plasterwork decoration at All Saints Church,
Ennismore Gardens, London, 1879-1903.

In 1904, when he was fifty-one, Sumner moved his wife and
five children, cat and one servant into the new house. All the
details of the acquisition of land, the building work and the
Sumners' removal may be found in the first chapter of this book.
Sumner relied on information from cottagers in the locality when
buying and adding to his land and used local firms to supply
materials made nearby, including Carter's of Poole for tiles and
briquettes, Monk of Ringwood for wrought-iron basket grates and
Sydenham of Poole for tongue-and-grooved oak floorboards. The
sand, gravel, paling and fencing all came from the Avon Valley
area of Hampshire. It is interesting to note that the house is also
well-known locally for having originally been equipped with pine
needle closets instead of flushing lavatories.

Cuckoo Hill lies between the New Forest and Cranborne
Chase in the parish of Ibsley, and the lively interest which Sumner
and his children took in the parish, with its Common and
smallholdings, meant that they were quick to make friends in the
locality. The Sumners were a close-knit family, who kept up a

regular correspondence. They would often write to each other when away with the news of the Forest folk. The tittle-tattle that they picked up on their visits to cottagers was a source of endless pleasure, and *Cuckoo Hill* has an entire chapter devoted to 'Cottage Chronicles', which shows the family's close involvement with the Thomases and the Hayters. Sumner writes of the Thomases that they 'were my first friends at Furze Hill . . . Their cottage has become a place of friendly resort for all the members of our household, and a gossip in Mrs Thomas' chimney corner is part of our life here'.

Sumner's prose enables us to picture the life of the smallholders in their mud-walled thatched cottages. The tasks of a farmer's wife included care of the family, housework, needlework, dairy work, fetching and carrying water from a well or a spring, building a fire with wood or peat, and, of course, cooking and baking bread. The small farmers also managed land, cattle, horses, pigs and poultry, and many kept a 'bee garden' on the Common. Sumner, who was as much a craftsman as an artist, was full of admiration for the little details of husbandry and craftsmanship which were manifest in the lives of his neighbours. James Bush's clipped yew hedges at Woodford Bottom, which were shaped into tight posy-like clusters of foliage, appear not only in an illustration in *Cuckoo Hill* but also in Sumner's wallpaper designs 'The Evergreen' and 'Springtime'. In his own garden, Sumner planted various species of apple trees – pippins, Cox's and codlings – from which he made pure apple juice, applying his customary care to its recipe. In this he was influenced by William Cobbett, whose *Cottage Economy* (1828) Sumner quotes in the chapter entitled 'Pomona'.

During his life in South Gorley, Sumner participated fully in the village life around him, and in 1906 he joined with the men of Ibsley in the controlled annual burning of the furze (gorse) that choked the surrounding Cuckoo and Furze Hills. This must have been a stunning as well as a frightening sight, for the illustrations to 'Heath Fires' are among the most dramatic in *Cuckoo Hill*.

A single storey, mud-walled cottage in the New Forest, *c.* 1900.

The people of Ibsley, however, were not always engaged in such innocent and public-spirited customs. Their closed community could also harbour secrets which Sumner discloses in 'Mutability'. This chapter includes a description of the smuggling runs from the nearby coast in which a supply of fresh horses, readily available in the New Forest, was essential to a speedy gang. Spirits and tea were the chief booty of the smugglers in the eighteenth and nineteenth centuries, and a keg of brandy found hidden in a stable was often the reward to collaborators.

In *Cuckoo Hill*, Sumner makes his reader aware of the sweep of history and of the way in which man has altered the shape of the land or has exploited its natural resources. This is why he so admired the ways of the Forest people, who, within their 'rights' or customs granted by the Crown, eked out a living from the soil. They dug sand and clay for agricultural purposes (Right of Marl) and turf for fuel (Right of Turbary); they collected wood (Right of Estovers), put their animals out to pasture (Right of Pasturing) and at prescribed periods took their pigs to eat acorns in the woods (Right of Pannage or Mast). There were also Fern Rights (the crop

Fern Gatherers at work in the New Forest, *c.* 1910.

was harvested in the Autumn and sold by the waggon-load as litter) and Hollying for which cutting began in November to supply traders at Christmas time. For all such rights the commoners made payment to the Crown and any disputes were settled by the Ancient Court of Verderers in Lyndhurst. Rights were granted not to individuals but to cottages or tenancies. Several of the rights still exist today.

Unlike the Forest, which belongs to the Crown, Cranborne Chase has always been owned by individuals, but it too had various customs for the preservation of 'vert and venison'. These are described by Sumner in his chapter on 'Cranborne Chase', which is informed by his vivid sense of history and an obvious desire to share the information that he has gathered on earlier inhabitants of the Chase area. He draws up a most readable history of the area, which places the Prehistoric, Roman, Romano-British, Anglo-Saxon and Medieval settlers in both chronological and geographical perspective, 'an honoured death-roll commemorated by long barrows and round barrows that still remain as land marks'. Sumner is also at pains to bring out the contrast between the landscapes of the Forest and Chase, relishing the 'great chalk uplands' of the latter. Although, as Sumner notes, Cranborne Chase has been disfranchised and most of the district is cultivated farmland, 'yet still it retains a character of spacious wildness'. Even today, looking out from the exposed, windswept ramparts of Badbury Rings on to rolling farmland, the same sense of space and of standing on the roof of the surrounding countryside predominates.

The Chase and the Forest, the high windswept ridges or the well-protected forest floor, these contrasting terrains continued to preoccupy Sumner during the second half of his life; by 1910 he had embarked on a self-imposed regime of recording the ancient earthworks and Roman pottery sites in his area. His inspiration was the work of General Pitt-Rivers. Encouraged by his friends, the archaeologists J.P. Williams Freeman and O.G.S. Crawford, and later collaborating with W.G. Wallace, Sumner systematically planned the earthworks of Cranborne Chase, the New Forest, and the Bournemouth district. He continued by carrying out a study of Romano-British pottery sites and kiln remains, which is probably his best-known work in archaeology. Working by himself Sumner had, by the age of seventy-two (1925), excavated and published papers on thirteen different sites. His crisp technical draughtsmanship is best appreciated in his maps and plans; they are stylized and ornamented by individual touches, reminiscent of his earlier black and white graphic work, carried out some forty years before.

In front of Cuckoo Hill, and running past Blunt's Barn, is Huckles Brook where groups of Forest ponies drink. A narrow road follows the brook up towards the Forest and where this terminates, Huckles Brook turns into Latchmore Brook (Sumner spells this Latchmoor). Here the road becomes a track, with various footpaths leading from it. On the south side of Latchmore Brook, the heathland is spongy underfoot and punctuated by grassy hummocks, clumps of gorse and patches of bracken or fern. The brook curves and chatters over a floor of bright amber-coloured

Pen and ink and watercolour drawing, *c.* 1921.

gravel: if it is followed towards its source for a couple of miles past Hasley Enclosure, Sloden Wood and Amberwood are reached. This is the very route that Sumner took on numerous occasions from about 1917 to 1925, either on foot or by bicycle, when he went to explore and excavate the Roman pottery sites at Sloden. In *Cuckoo Hill* he mentions that there was a thriving pottery industry in this now deserted place, and by following the potters' footsteps Sumner was to bring their ghosts to life.

Of the many remarkable projects undertaken by Sumner at South Gorley, the production of the manuscript called *Cuckoo Hill* must surely remain his most extraordinary. Playfully named 'my elderly hobbies' it is a sidelong look at his life and times, a personal journal and yet a guide: a book of history, customs, topography and nature. Sumner wrote and illustrated three volumes of manuscript. The first volume, on which this book is based, contains a host of charming and atmospheric watercolour illustrations that complement the text and tell us much about the region at the beginning of the century, not only the shape of the landscape but the type of planting, the position of the roads and tracks and the changes of light.

The method by which Sumner matched words to illustrations in *Cuckoo Hill* is not recorded but it seems likely that he wrote out his script in pen and ink first and left regular gaps to which he would return and illustrate with pencil and watercolour. (In several cases these gaps remained permanently unfilled.) These illustrations are a pivotal point in the development of Sumner's style. They are almost like maquettes (a sculptor's small preliminary model), rather than sketches, for full-size works. Their format relates exactly to the double-page spread of the small bound sketch books which Sumner always used, but their treatment is much tighter and more studied than most of his sketch book entries. Each watercolour is a painting in itself, carefully worked out in the quiet of the library at Cuckoo Hill from sketches and colour notes that were blended together with Sumner's visual memory.

Heywood Sumner's life went full circle: from his rural beginnings in the Hampshire countryside to his demanding city life and back again. He chose the New Forest landscape to give him nourishment in his maturity, and the record that he left behind of this his private world is enjoyable and enlightening. His writing is weighed and descriptive: it is imbued with an artist's vision, a topographer's knowledge and an archaeologist's curiosity. The delightful illustrations, the cameos of local characters, the descriptions of regional skills and practices, the odd spellings and dialects that lace the story of *Cuckoo Hill*, all combine to capture a

A winter scene in the New Forest, *c.* 1900.

special sense of place. Sumner has left us with a picture of a corner of England that is evocative, idiosyncratic and unique.

Heywood Sumner's house, Cuckoo Hill, still shelters beneath the steep slopes of Furze and Cuckoo Hills, which are part of Ibsley Common and which back on to the Forest. Below the house the land falls away to a plain through which run the main road between Fordingbridge and Ringwood and the River Avon. A bluish haze marks out the tree-lined river and masks the rising slopes of Cranborne Chase away to the west, where the sun sets. Sumner was moved to write in *Cuckoo Hill*, 'Whatever changes and chances life may have in store for us, I do say my grace most devoutly for having found this beautiful place and for having accomplished this piece of work'.

Heywood Sumner died in seclusion at Cuckoo Hill in 1940, less than a year after his wife Agnes's death and soon after the outbreak of the Second World War; he was eighty-seven years old.

Margot Coatts, 1987

Based upon the Ordnance Survey Map

# A Map of Ancient Sites in the New Forest Cranborne Chase & Bournemouth District

Scale. 2 miles to 1 inch.

## Symbols.

∴ Round barrows. — Long barrows
● Defensive Camps. ═══ and Dykes
◉ Pastoral Enclosures. ══ Dykes of debatable purpose.
◎ Romano British villages.
▲ Roman villas. ◆ & Pottery kiln sites.
+ Roman finds. ♜ Norman Castles.

Black = Pre-Roman. Red = Roman.
Green = Post Roman. — Numerals in-dicate land altitudes above the sea

Heywood Sumner. 1922.

Green bands mark New Forest bound-ary of A.D. 1300. & Cranborne Chase out-bounds of A.D. 1618

At Buttsash and Langley, 'street' place name in New Forest Perambulations support the Roman road tradition, but excavation evidence is wanting.

The New Forest.

The Solent.

Isle of Wight.

The Book

of Gorley
by Heywood Sumner.

1905.

Gorley means the open forest place where cattle lie ; & this book is a chronicle, written at leisure, of the making of our new home on Cuckoo Hill at South Gorley, & of the life that surrounds us here, at the edge of the New Forest.

Under the greenwood tree
Who loves to lie with me,
And tune his merry note
Unto the sweet bird's throat —
Come hither, come hither, come hither!
    Here shall we see
    No enemy
But winter and rough weather.


Who doth ambition shun
And loves to live i' the sun,
Seeking the food he eats
And pleased with what he gets —
Come hither, come hither, come hither!
    Here shall he see
    No enemy
But winter and rough weather.

# Cuckoo Hill.

Midway between Fordingbridge & Ringwood, the
Avon leaves its habitual course through meadows liable
to floods, & flows for a few hundred yards beside the
Salisbury & Bournemouth highway. On one side is
the river, spanned by a stone bridge, shaded by old
elms, on the other side stand a few thatched cottages,
& this is Ibsley or Ibsley street as the villagers
call it.
In the year 1882 I was doing some etchings for
Sotheran's edition of Wise's New Forest, and, after
a spring day spent in wandering about Fordingbridge,
chance & the good highway brought me tired and

homeless to Ibsley. Here I determined to stay: but where? for there is no inn to the street. So I knocked at the first cottage door, ' Could I have a night's lodging?' - 'No' - The next - 'No' - & so on, all along the row of thatched homes that makes Ibsley street so attractive to the passer-by. At last I got into conversation with one of these negative cottage dames, &, I suppose, reassured her as to my good faith, for eventually she agreed to give me both bed & board, while after supper she confided that the cause of my curt refusal by her neighbours was — they thought that I was a robber. At the time I attributed this either to my natural appearance or to the wild life that prevailed at the edge of the Forest. Now, however, I know it was owing to a mild robbery that had just occurred at the Rectory, & any stranger was accordingly suspect.
And this was my first introduction to Ibsley.

Years afterwards, in 1897, we went to Bournemouth owing to Agnes' ill-health. At first merely for a change, but eventually a return to London was agreed to be unadviseable, & so 'Skerryvore' was taken where we lived for 6 years.
If ever there was a garden city, Bournemouth is the place, for it is made up of miles & miles of houses in gardens; another little house in another little garden, & then another little house in another

-2-

Cuckoo Hill.

little garden, & so on & so on, nearly all the way from Christ
Church to Poole. I never loved the sea, & did not find refreshment in garden city life : but the country inland was a
constant joy : I used to bicycle about a great deal in
those days, 40, 50, & 60 mile rides : & so it came to
pass that I knew all the country round Bournemouth,
& revived all my old acquaintance with the Forest :
went to Boldrewood Farm : stayed at Highwood
Farm : wandered about Burley with Captain Elwes:
got to know about the buying & selling of land round
the Forest, & how hard it was to get a good site, &
thus I began the dream of possession.
Then Agnes' health at Bournemouth furthered the process
of uprooting. She made no progress there. The health-
-giving of the place seemed to be used up. So what with

○ Jame's, here we spent our honeymoon, September 1883.

.3.

my own inclinations & her health, I passed from dream to action, & set about discovery in real earnest.

My aim was to find a squatter's holding on the gravel hills of the Forest between Ringwood & Fordingbridge, where we could begin by making the experiment of life in a cottage amid wild air, & my first attempt was made at Gonville Farm which stands on Gorley Hill beside Hungerford copse But Dr Rake of Fordingbridge, the owner, was not inclined to sell, so I wandered over Gorley Hill to Furze Hill & got talking to Mrs John Thomas at their farm-yard gate. When she knew what I wanted, she said, 'she'd tell father' & he'd write to me'; so he did ; nothing for sale about Furze hill, but there might be, etc _ Then I went over to see John Thomas, & found out that Charles Tayler of Cuckoo Hill might be open to an offer for his tumble down cottage & 2½ acres of meadow & orchard.

I made the mistake of deputing John Thomas to sound him, instead of doing so myself ; result ; Nil. Then Frampton of Ringwood was suggested _ he might sell two fields _ Paradise by name _ 2½ acres again I deputed John Thomas ; result ; Nil . Then Thomas told me of Davy's site at Linch near Becky's drove _ Davy _ a retired Ringwood solicitor _ lived down in Somersetshire, so I wrote to him ; result ; no

Adlams

reply. Finally, I did what I ought to have done before.
—went to Charles Hayter & had it out with him.

Since I had begun to look about for a site, two
things had happened. I had quite decided that Cuckoo
Hill was the place that I wanted; & Hayter's cottage
had suffered further from winter storms. It was ⋮⋮
mud-walled; 60 years old; & built moreover by a
shoe-maker —Day — who would have done better to
have stuck to his last, for his walls now only stood
with assistance, trigged up by means suitable for
over-laden apple-trees. The cottage was plainly
tumbling down, & something would have to be done,
so Charles Hayter's disposition was changed —he was
open to an offer. Then I found that he had only a

life interest in the property, his son being the ultimate free-holder — 'Could he see his son, & talk over my offer to purchase?' — 'Perhaps he could, but his son lived at :·: Buckland Newton in Dorsetshire, & the carrier only went there twice a week from Dorchester, so it would take him 3 days to get there & back again' — This journey of 30 miles by rail, & of 8 miles by road was a serious under — taking; but eventually it was decided that Charles Hayter would go to see his son, & discuss the matter with him.

When he returned, I came over to hear the result of his expedition.

Charles Hayter stood inside his gate. I stood outside. We both talked cautiously about things that neither of us had met to talk about, & then slowly came to the point — 'What did your son say?' — 'No, it won't, I tell 'ee it won't do, my son mid agree, but we ain't agoing to agree as to price' — & so on, evidently with private wrath inspiring his words; at length he came to the price upon which we weren't agoing to agree — £200 — £150 I suggest-ed, & at this the private wrath was made public in a vigorous attack upon John Thomas — 'John Thomas, he told 'ee that price, he's too sharp, he wants something out of 'en for hisself, & it won't do, I tell 'ee, it won't do, he's too sharp'. I never quite made out the inner history of this thunder-clap that had surely been long gathering & suddenly

The Beginning.

outburst, but when the storm of words was over, Charles Hayter resumed his natural deliberation, & after a long discussion we agreed on £175 as the price, while I was to pay Thomas £5 for his help in the matter . Charles Hayter & his daughter, (Miss Hayter of dress-making fame) were to remain in the cottage till Michaelmas, while I was to be given possession of the field at Lady-day .

    So the purchase was settled March 18. 1902 . The site was difficult, most sites are I suppose, any-now, the outflow of spring water from the hillside, the variety of soil, & the fall of the ground all needed a great deal of consideration

    Probably, if I had to build it again, as it is now, enlarged ; I should shift the site some yards southward. When planning the first part of the house, I specially kept a 'Prophet' apple-tree near the garden porch way for Hayter's praise of 'they Prophets' was in the highest. But now that the house is enlarged, it comes too near the fine oak on the North side beside the dining-room window. However, the apples are good. They Prophets deserve their praise; & I can smoke a pipe with peace as I reconsider the plan from Gorley Hill.

The approximate estimate for the first part of the house was £550, but this did not include any of the outbuildings, road work, cistern, water supply or terrace. The house actually cost £700. The outside work mentioned above came to £216. The common supplied shingle for concrete, red gravel for the roads, yellow & silver sand for mortar & rough-cast. The bricks came from Blissford. The road making was begun in the middle of May, & the foundations were laid at the end of May, 1902 - W.E. Alexander of Ringwood was the builder; George Pilley was the foreman; & the work went on steadily, but short-handed for 10 months.

During the progress of the building, I realized that Samuel Phipotts' field — Townsend ground, adjoining Hayter's — was necessary to me in the possible event of the house having to be enlarged, &, as he was willing to sell, it was merely a question of price. £200 was his figure, & he was immoveable; so this was bought February 18. 1903. & 2¼ more acres added to Cuckoo Hill.

Cuckoo Hill from the path to Ibsley

On April 3. 1903. Beatrix, Clara, Barnes & I inhabited the new house at Cuckoo Hill for the first time.
On April 7. Agnes, Doris, Humphrey & Christopher joined us : Michael completing the party on April 8.

During the summer of 1903 Agnes was in better health than she had been for some years past ; so we :∵ decided to add to the house, to sell or let 'Skerryvore', & to make Cuckoo Hill our permanent home.

With this end in view, I sold the kitchen garden at 'Skerryvore' to Mr Lewis for £425, & then bought the two Paradise fields from Frampton of Ringwood for £380 —just in time, for he had actually ordered the bricks for a house to be built near the stile. These fields contain $6\frac{1}{2}$ acres, are good land, but were very foul when I bought them, having been quite neglected for years past.

Then in August I made a road up to the house from the Blunt's Barn lane, so as to avoid the steep 'le-ane' hill, & thus began the building of the second part of the house.

The addition works did not at first interfere with our domestic arrangements. In September however I was away, completing the wall-decoration at All Saints:: Ennismore Gardens, but Agnes stayed on with the children until October 26.

Then 'Eagle's Nest' on the Westcliff, Bournemouth was taken for 3 months, & there Agnes had a severe illness which kept her abed most of the time.

In January 1904 we got possession of 'Skerryvore' — which had been let meantime to Mr Meade, furnished; & now relet, unfurnished, to Mr Gataker for 7. or 10 years — then we packed up, & cleared out by January 21, & I went over to Cuckoo Hill to unload the vans.

Their arrival was memorable. They were delayed on the road, & did not reach Gorley till 4. o'clock. Then they stuck in the clay of the 'le-ane' hill. Immoveably. There was nothing to be done but to unload them:: there. So Peggy was put in the cart, & all the workmen on the job, & everyone in Gorley came to help. So, by the light of a frosty moon, & of stable lanthorns our household gods were conveyed in long processions to

.1903.                                    The original house.

the unfinished house. Then followed a month of going
to & fro, till finally on February 16. 1904. Agnes
Beatrix, Christopher, & Blackmore came from ∵∴
Bournemouth in a snowstorm, & we were fairly sett-
-led in.

The building of the second part of the house, with
the outside work, road-making, barn & shed, gates
etc, came to £1100

Blunt's Barn, & the field of 3½ acres adjoining
were bought in October 1904. They belonged to George
Thomas, & he, being a sharp trader, saw his opportunity
fixed his price at £500, & enforced it by a scheme — which
I knew he could & would carry out — of building a
barrack row of brick & slate cottages near the barn.
This field was quite indispensable for the completion of
my little holding, as it gave me Lord Normanton & the

.11.

Common as my adjoining neighbours on all four sides.
So there was nothing to be done but to pay his price with
as good a grace as I could command. The bargain
was struck up at Hyde, in George Thomas' house, &
he threw in 6 smuggled cigars as good-luck. The barn
is said to have been built 200 years ago, & is in perfectly
good structural repair.

The servant's hall wing was added in the spring
of 1905, & at the same time I got a lease from Lord
Normanton of 'Cuckoo's Hill garden', & of Shutler's piece
—the latter being specially useful as back premises for
the wood & coal shed, which was re-erected there, on
its present site.

The stable & coach-house barn was built in May
& June of the same year. All its framework timbers are
of sweet chestnut, & I followed the example of Blunt's
Barn in the weather-boarding of un-edged elm boards.
These additions cost £394.


So we made our new home at Cuckoo Hill after many
wanderings, & here we have found good health & are
making roots which I hope will maintain & retain our
family tree for many years. Indeed, whatever changes
& chances Life may have in store for us, I do say my
grace most devoutly for having found this beautiful

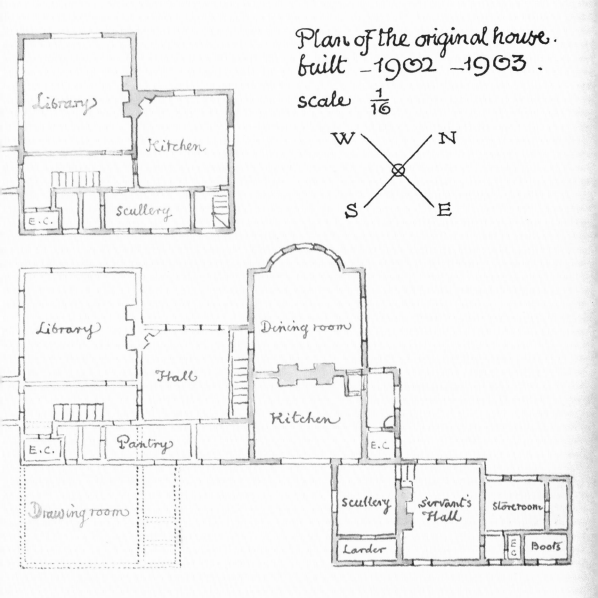

Plan of the original house.
built —1902 —1903.
scale 1/16

W N
⊗
S E

Plan of the house with additions of 1904.
1905.
The dotted lines show the position of the
intended drawing-room.

place, & for having accomplished this piece of work .
Sit Laus Deo .


## Notes .

The robbery at Ibsley Rectory, referred to on p.2 was ::
perpetrated on Mr Jenkins, then curate in charge. The thie[f]
took a pocket case of communion plate, & hid it in the
avenue between Ibsley & Ellingham Cross, where it was
recovered : also a pair of trowsers, in which he was captured.

The water Supply comes from 2 constant springs of good
soft water. One for drinking & for the bath-room, by the
entrance to the old cottage , the other, on the common
above the stile leading into Paradise . An iron pipe
running under the house takes the water from this spring
into a cement tank by the front entrance, whence it
is pumped up into the house cistern.

The rough cast 'splatter-cash' was gauged 3 sand to
1 of Portland cement , then 7 of this was mixed with
2 of run lime , the latter being added so as to make th[e]
plaster 'fat' for the pebbles which were flung on in
handfuls & then pressed in with a float.    The
brickwork at the angles was cut to a splay, so as to
avoid making a corner or aris of roughcast .

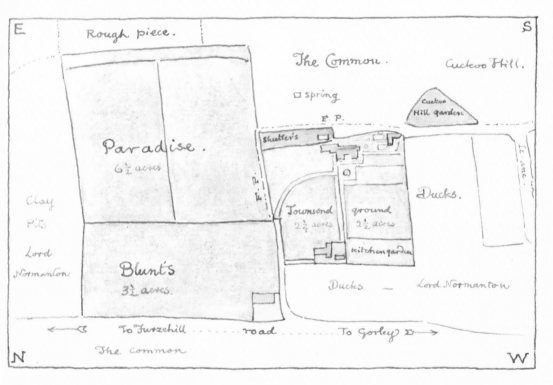

E     Rough piece.            S

The Common.      Cuckoo Hill.

□ spring

Cuckoo Hill garden

F. P.

Shutter's

Paradise.
6½ acres

Clay Pits

Lord Normanton

Townsend
2¾ acres

ground
2½ acres

Ducks.

kitchen garden

Blunt's
3½ acres.

Ducks  —  Lord Normanton

To Furzehill ....... road ....... To Gorley

The common

N                         W

General Plan of buildings & fields — The green shows freehold, bluegreen leased.

The croquet ground terrace was made in the winter of 1904 1905, & cartloads of clay were removed & dumped in the shingle pit on Cuckoo Hill — There is a deep trench dug at the base of the upper bank, filled in with large stones & shingle, with a fall to the boundary ditch of 'Ducks'. In the early part of 1905 I was dis-appointed with the result, for after rain, water stood on the lawn, Then we had a dry summer; &, I suppose, the worms worked down to the water at the bottom of the deep trench, anyhow, when the rain fell in the late autumn, it drained off immediately, & the worm castings testified to their presence.

The final addition — for it really is final so far as I am
concerned — was begun in December 1905, & was
completed in July 1906. During this time I was away
at St. John's Miles Platting from January 1st to March,
making two week-end visits to see the work in progress.
There was a great deal of preliminary earth moving
to be done at the back, some of the excavated clay
was used to increase the width of the croquet ground
terrace, while the rest was dumped on the common
— near the stile leading into Paradise. George Pilley
was again the foreman, &, as before, the work proceeded
without hindrance. Deacon, of Blissford, supplied the
bricks at 33/6 a thousand — 1/6 more than delivered at

the bottom of the hill — Ballam of Creekmoor, Poole,
again supplied the tiles & grooved bricks & floor
squares; & Carter's of Poole supplied the briquettes
& tiles for the mantelpieces & hearths — The wrought
iron basket grates throughout, were made by Monk,
who is a working blacksmith at Ringwood.

Sydenham, of Poole, supplied the oak floor-boards
for the drawing-room; they were laid on 5"×2" joists,
16" apart, resting on 5 sleeper walls, these latter being
4'.10" apart. The floor-boards are 4" wide by $\frac{9}{10}$" thick,
tongued & grooved, & secret nailed.

This addition cost £560 — making a total of £2964. for the
building, roads, etc, & £1255. for the land & Blunts Barn.

Great Chibden bottom

.18.

## The Common.

There is a forest track leading from the Royal Oak
at Fritham to Mockbeggar, & those who take this way
pass over a plain of scattered hollies on Hiscock's Hill,
through ancient woods of oak & yew & whitebeam
at Sloden, across miles of rugged heathland, past Hasley
past Ogden's purlieu, past Whitefield Clumps, till the
gravel hills abruptly dip, the heather stops, the Avon
valley begins, & the Forest limit is reached.

    So it seems.    But really the Forest boundary
lies more than a mile back, across the traversed plain.
There, on the edge of the gravel plateau, you may find

bound-posts if you search for them — The marking stakes of the old perambulations — Few, & far between — Low grey posts, furred with lichen, & hidden with ling, but declaring with immemorial authority, that here the Forest ends, & Ibsley Common begins — According to the custom of men = but not according to the habits of the beasts, the birds, & the green things that fulfill the days of Forest Creation; for they gain their scanty living where & how they can; alert, tenacious, & timid yet without respect for the posts, nor of their customary bounds; for they — like the way-farer — only recognise the limit imposed by cultivation.

The Crown & the Commoners however have agreed differently: So the wild expanse of unbroken Forest land has been divided by an unmarked line that stretches from post to post: that separates Forest rights from Common rights: & that says in defiance of Nature's contradiction, but with the authority of the Ordnance Survey map — — Here the Forest ends, & Ibsley Common begins —

There is no doubt now as to the boundaries be-tween the Forest & the Common: but if we turn to the Perambulations of the New Forest made in the 29th year of Edward I, & in the 22nd year of Charles II, we find that some encroachment would seem to have been made since then, either by the Lord of the Manor, or by the Commoners of Ibsley; though the old place names are sufficiently dubious to give zest to their identification, & uncertainty as to my conclusions. Here, side by side for comparison, are the two Perambulations, from Rockford common at the Southern extremity to Coliford at the Northern

## Perambulations.

| Edward. I. | Charles. II. |
|---|---|
| And so to Rodeneshined And so descending as far as Dockeneswater unto the Markingstak. And from thence into Wythladeslak. And thence unto Merkinbregh above :: Gorlyngesdon. And from thence directly unto the Putts in :: Merkynggeslade And from thence to Derlygh And so unto Celiares fled. | And from thence going down :: by a little vale called Rodenbottome to Illbridge upon a water called Dockenwater. And from thence to Mockinborough upon Gorlesdowne alias Gorley Hill. And so across a place called Gorley Hill to Pits. And from thence to :: Charlesford alias Coliarsford. |

The marking line that crosses the two brooks — the Dockens water at Illbridge, & the Hucklesbrook at Coliford — is the same now as then. 'Wythladeslak' I suppose to be on the plain now called Whitefield : 'Merkinbregh', 'Mockinborough', to be Mockbeggar : 'Gorlyngesdon', 'Gorlesdowne alias Gorley Hill' would seem to be the Summerlug & Shab hill ridges which lead up to the sand stone pits at the top of Brogenslade. 'Merkynggeslade' may be Brogenslade, while 'Derlygh' may be Dorridge. 'And from thence to Derlygh And so unto Celiaresford  Charlesford alias Coliarsford (now Coliford) identifies the crossing of the Huckles brook, & confirms my supposition that the hill now called Gorley Hill was not 'Gorlyngesdon, Gorlesdowne alias Gorley Hill of the Perambulations.

To a stranger this separation between a waste of heath land called Common, & a similar waste called Forest must seem to be merely the difference between Tweedledum & Tweedledee; but it is not so regarded by the Commoners, for the Ibsley common rights are much more worth having than Forest rights. For example Common rights allow me, as a freeholder in the parish, to turn out as many beasts as I like without payment; to dig as much gravel, sand, or soil, & to cut as much turf, gorse, fern, or heath as I require — provided that it is for my own use in the parish; & , I suppose, with the reservation that the user must be 'reasonable', though hitherto this point of 'reasonable' user has not been raised here — On the other hand a Commoner may not cut a tree on the Common, but he may pull one up — a distinction which prevents the Lord of the Manor from planting trees on the common against the will of the Commoners

A Commoner has no right to shoot nor to fish, nor may he dig sandstone — of which there is a pit at the top of ::
Brogenslade. [Query. 'Pits' of Chas II. Peran.bulation.]

Forest rights on the other hand are more restricted. They are of four different kinds. Rights of pasturage which allow you to turn out ponies at 1/6 ahead — or I should perhaps say a-tail, as they are tailmarked — & cows at 2/, payable in both cases to the marksman. Rights of mast, which allow you to turn out pigs at 2ᵈ each. Rights of turf, which allow you to cut a specified number of turves without payment: And Rights of Sign wood — or assign wood — which give you the right to so many cords of wood in the Forest.

These rights belong to holdings & to houses, & if a house has rights of sign wood, & the house is pulled down, the rights are lost; a chimney must be kept standing to retain them.

Every place has its antiquities, yet to write of the antiquities of the Common may suggest the inversion of ancient & modern; for the most ancient barrows & marks on the Common are new compared with its own essential permanence. Above Newtown & on Dorridge the "humpy grounds" record some honoured Keltic burial, but the great features of the Common were old when these barrows were new: plain, whale-back hills, & hollows like the troughs of ocean rollers, tell of primæval seas, of upheaval from sea-floor to dry land, & of down-rushing rains in the dim years of unaccountable period; & all the change that chance & Time have wrought on the Common has merely resulted in furrows that have deepened on its old face, & in hills more rounded beneath the elements. Indeed the marks of man, either in life or death, are scanty on this abiding wild. The turf-cutter's spade still leaves its oval scar on the peaty ground: North Hollow pit yearly increases its sunken semicircle of red gravel: In autumn the cut fern tells of the thrifty commoner, & the gun-shot of the Lord of the Manor; while all the year round solitary figures seek for strayed cattle & ponies — like Saul sought for the lost asses of Kish — otherwise the plains & hills and bottoms retain their wild silence, & the habitual solitude of centuries continues. Possibly its solitude has increased. Certainly the trackways over the Common must have been more used in the British & Roman days when the potters were plying their trade at Sloden, & traffic to & from these potteries must have helped to make the deep 'drokes', or sunken ways, that lead up to, & down from the plain on the North & the South sides. In later times, Tradition handed on from father to son — James Flayter to wit — maintains that a hollow near the green track from Cuckoo

.24.

Hill to Robin Hood's clump was made for a cockpit, & here cock-fighting might be enjoyed without disturbance. While below, in Chibden bottom, there are three banked up rings which mark the sites of 'bee-gardens' — places where beehives were put out when the heather bloomed, & where the bees were looked after by some beekeeping commoner. This seems to have been customary on the North side of the Forest, & Hive Garn — or garden — is a place name near Ashley, that testifies to the custom.

The three clumps of Scots Fir & Weymouth pine — Whitefield Robin Hood's, & Dorridge — were planted by the 2$^{nd}$ Lord Normanton to give landmarks & variety to his view of the long line of the New Forest Hills from Somerley — so the story is told — Whitefield & Dorridge were planted about 1835 — Robin Hood's about 1850 — Dorridge is the highest ground on the Common — 257 feet above the sea level — while the lowest part is at the cattle stop, where the Huckles brook leaves the Common — 100 feet above the sea level.

And now from places I turn to names — There is a con-stant pleasure in place-name enquiry, & here as else-where the names on the common give scope for per--plexity & supposition. Amateur etymology probably ends, as it begins, with a note of interrogation; but at least the question is intelligent, & though I may be wrong in my suggestions, yet some one else may thereby be aroused to a better understanding & arrive at a truer interpretation

Great Chibden & Little Chibden bottoms are on either side of Shab hill. Shab means _rough_ It seems possible that the name Chibden is a perversion of Shabden _the rough hollow. <sup>Q? Joan Shabden was a parishioner of Ibsley in 1690 perhaps a personal place name</sup>

Dorridge may be Dunridge _ hill fort ridge _ just as Durham was Dunholm, softened on Norman lips to Duresme (Isaac Taylor). On the other hand Durham is derived by Bosworths Anglo-Saxon dictionary from Deorham _ The abode of wild-beasts _ Deor being A.S. for an animal wild beasts _ deer. & so Dorridge may be deer ridge; or dark ridge from A.S. Deore, or again The renowned place of a corpse, from Deore _beloved, renowned _ & lic _a corpse In support of this last is Derlygh as it is spelt in the Perambulation of Edward I; are the barrows on the hill, & also the name Latchmoor belonging to the neighbouring valley leading up to Fritham, Latch or Lich being derived from Lic (e.g Lichgate.) see Wise's New Forest. p.199.

Whitefield is rather a puzzling place-name, as white is not the colour suggested by a heath-clad moor. Nevertheless White field, Whitemoor, White shoot & White hill are common names in the Forest. e.g Whitefieldmoor

Ladywell droke

near Ober Farm — White moor, near Berry Beeches, near Milla
Ford bridge, near Lyndhurst race-course, near Stinchelsea
& on Rockford common — White shoot (hill) on Sloden,
near Halliday's Hill cottage, & on Hiscocks Hill — White
bridge Hill, near Ironshill enclosure etc — There are
however two self-asserting white products of the moor
— stones, & cotton-grass in June flower — The top
gravel stones on heathland are always bleached for
a foot or two downwards by the tannic acid that is
washed from the heath roots, & this surely accounts for
the White shoot (hill) place names, as the gravelly
tracks on the heather hills are gleaming white land-
-marks from afar : while if you have seen the cotton
grass waving its feathery white tassels & shining amid

North Hollow Bridge

the rusty green of the bogs you will at once recognise the
the reason of the Whitemoor names. Whitefield however
remains unsuggestive as a place-name, for it is a plain
of plateau gravel, clad with heath, Furze & Fern; the two
tracks leading up to Whitefield from Linwood certainly
are white shoots (hills) & perhaps the plain got its

name from the tracks that give access to it. <u>Linwood</u>
may be Lime wood — Lyndhurst is thus derived by Isaac
Taylor*. <u>Huckles brook</u> — query, diminutive from huck
a hook, a brook of little bends — a description that certainly applies — <u>Dockens water</u>. query, from A. S.
deag, deóg, — dark, solitary — <u>Droke</u>, old trackways

that lead on to the common are locally called `drokes` — this may come from A.S. dragan, drōg, to drag, to proceed. Brogenslade. Query — A.S. brogden, varie-gated, slade is a little valley between wooded hills. In place, it seems to correspond with the Merkynggeslade of Edward I. Perambulation. Which oddly spelt name suggests a `Markingstak` origin. Brown's Castle above Newtown, & Sander's Castle above Furze Hill merely record hills specially used by neighbouring turf cutters. Brown used to live in Noyce's cottage; Sanders in Stephen Shutler's, so I am told, — Lucas' Castle & Thompson's Castle in Latchmoor are similar place names, & this personal origin of forest names must often be supposed. Tommy Goff's bridge over the Docken's water & Sharles lane leading up to North hollow gravel pit are instances. — Goff now lives on a small Freehold adjoining the Linwood road — Sharles used to live in Marlow's cottage & made the lane in question, so says Stephen Shutler.

Ill bridge is one of the old place names on the common, it crosses the Docken's water between North Hollow bridge & Tommy Goff's bridge, & is mentioned in the Perambulation of Charles II. Probably Ill merely describes the badness of the bridge — it now consists of one log across the water. If however you prefer to be ingenious, there is the A.S. Il — a hedge-hog from which to derive it, though the connection may not carry conviction —

.30.

Summer Lug Hill above Mockbeggar

Leaden-hall. Query: F.S. Leden, Roman hill. (There is also Leaden hall above Cockly Plain, both are near the Roman-British potteries)

North Hollow gravel pit, mentioned on the last page, has the reputation of supplying the best gravel hereabouts. It is rich golden brown in colour, & has enough clay in its substance to make it bind well. The gravel at ∴ Mockbeggar pit is of a much more shingly nature & poorer in colour. This mixture of clay with the plateau gravel of our hill-tops, & the consequent slow filtration of the rainfall, probably account for the constancy of our springs. Like Charity, they never fail. In the driest summer, when the springs at Hungerford & Hyde have been parched to death, & when our brook has ceased to flow, the springs on Ibsley common will still be running with curious persistance. Yet it is traditional, this drought in the valleys & water on the hills. 'Jack & Jill went up a hill to fetch a pail of water'. So do we. On this side of the common the water comes out just about the 200 feet line; & if you look along our hills you will notice a a change of colour in the heather, running like a ruled line along their sides: above, the ling grows finely; below, the cross leaved heath & strap-grass dwindle in sour patches, & this change marks where the subsoils differ — where

.31.

the gravel ends & the clay begins, & where water will surely be found — The highest springs on the common are Lady-well, & the source of Great Chibden Gutter on the upper side of Shab Hill. On the Linwood side — Lady-well excepted — the water comes out of the hills at a much lower level than on our side, & Linwood bog, beside the Docken's water, marks the outflow — Linwood bog, white with sheets of waving cotton grass in June, then starred with bog asphodel that turns from brimstone yellow to deep gold as it ripens its spike of seed vessels, scented with sweet-gale, haunted by snipes & plovers, channelled with little peaty gutters that drip into the Docken's water all through the long Midsummer days of drought between rusty tussocks of coarse bents & sulfur patches of quaking moss — Here is the cause of the Docken's water, & of its flow when the Huckle's brook on the other side of the hill is as dry as the brook Cherith: for when summer parches old Mother Earth, the overflow of our hill springs is sucked up by the thirsty land long before it can reach the distant brook.

Both these streams, with their gravelly strands over which the clear water runs amber & gold, seem as though they must be haunted by spawning salmon; but they are not; although the great fish come up the Avon as far as Fordingbridge, they do not now turn aside on the way. Twenty years ago — No, it must be more than

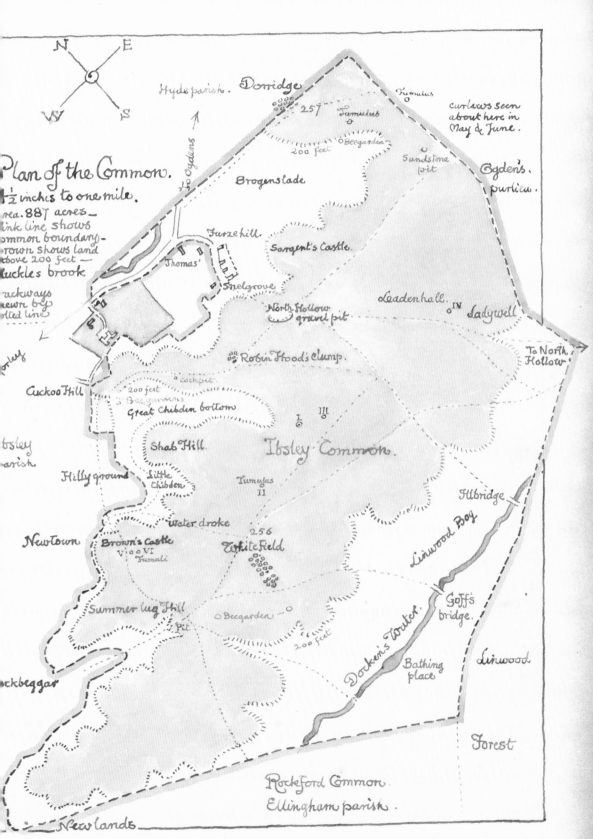

Plan of the Common.

1½ inches to one mile.

Area. 887 acres.

Thick line shows common boundary. Brown shows land above 200 feet. Huckles brook

Trackways shewn by dotted line

N E S W

Hyde parish. Dorridge

curlews seen about here in May & June.

257

Tumulus

Tumulus

Ogden's purlieu.

Beegarden

200 feet

Sandstone pit

To Ogdens

Brogenslade

Furze hill.

Sargent's Castle.

Thomas'

Snelgrove

Leadenhall

IV Ladywell

North Hollow gravel pit

To North Hollow

Robin Hood's clump.

cockpit

Cuckoo Hill

200 feet
Beegardens

Great Chibden bottom

I III

Shab Hill.

Ibsley Common.

Ibsley parish

Hilly ground

Little Chibden

Tumulus II

Illbridge

Newtown

Water droke

256

Brown's Castle V VI Tumuli

White Field

Linwood Bog

Summer Lug Hill

pit

Beegarden

200 feet

Docken's Water

Goff's bridge.

Linwood

Bathing place

ckbeggar

Forest

Rockford Common. Ellingham parish.

Newlands

.33.

that, the Salmon used to spawn up along these Forest stream
& a story is told here how a great 20 pound fish was
caught one Sunday morning, just below the cattle-stop
near Blunt's Barn; but when the powder mills were
first started at Eyeworth in 18    the water of the
Ffucklesbrook was fouled, the cattle would not drink
it, & the fish floated dead in the stream; this nuisance
has been stopped long ago, but though the water has run
clear for many years, the Salmon have never returned, and
even small fish are scarce. The Docken's water is fairly
supplied with small trout, & kingfishers haunt this stream
while they are only rarely to be seen on the Ffucklesbrook

The wild animal life on the common is much the same
as that to be found in the Forest. Roaming fallow
see Note
page 168* deer are occasionally to be seen; foxes have earths at
Foxholes above Brogenslade, on the South side, and
at Shab Hill — where I have seen one — hares are few
rabbits plentiful, in spite of the stoats who may often
be seen hunting them; partridges & pheasants out-lie
from the preserves in the valley; curlews come up from
the sea in May for nesting; snipes are plentiful in
Linwood bog, and occasionaly on our brook, near Shutle
copse; wild duck nest in Great Chibden bottom, &
in May they walk their brood down the' le-ane

.34.

to the Ffuckles brook & so on to the Avon; great is
the quacking fuss & frabble if they are interrupted in
their Exodus; Night-jars abound in May & June,
& glow worms light up on Cuckoo Ffill in July
when the Night-jars have ceased to churr; grass
snakes are common & adders rare; we have also the
smooth snake (Coronella austriaca), it is peculiar to the
New Forest & the heath land south of the Avon; a very
large one, 3 feet in length, was killed on our front drive;
this smooth snake is harmless, but hisses & darts in a
way that suggests venom _ Slow-worms are common _

Besides the birds already mentioned, I have seen the
following on the common & in our garden. White
owl. Brown owl. Heron _ Kestrel _ Great green wood-
pecker. Cuckoo. Whinchat. Lark. Fieldfare. Thrush. Missel
thrush. Blackbird. Rook (when the rooks come up on the
common, Stephen Shutlers says there will be rain.) Plover
Pheasant. Partridge. Magpie. Jay _ Green Finch. Goldfinch
Bulfinch. Chaffinch. Linnet. Chiff chaff. Nightingale
robin _ Red backed Shrike. Nuthatch. Wryneck (Cuckoo's
mate) Blue Tit. Long-tailed Tit. Wren. Swallow. Marten
Swift. Fly-catcher. Grey-wag tail. yellow-hammer. Water
Wag tail _ yellow Wag tail _ Willow wren _ Tree Creeper
Starling. Stone Chat. Sparrow. Ffedge-Sparrow _
Wood-pigeon _ Rock-Dove. Willow-Wren or Warbler

.35.

List of birds continued.  — King-fisher. Sea-gull (on

plough-land beside the Common.)


Note. Curlews are newcomers here — within the last 4 years — —
Note. There is fine hedgerow timber on the South & West sides
of the Common — mostly oak on the hills, & elm in the valley —
This timber owes its existence to a custom of the 2$^{nd}$ Lord Normanton, who always gave 1$^{d}$ per plant to the hedgers on
his property, when they left a well-grown young tree in
making (cutting & laying,) the fences — The present Lord Normanton
is benefitting, but if the trees continue to be felled at the same
rate as they have been recently, this beautiful feature of our hills &
valleys will only remain as a memory —

Whitefield Clump & Shab Hill

List of Plants found on the Common.

Furze - Ulex Europœa - Flowers February to May.

Dwarf Furze - Ulex Nana - Flowers August to November.

Needle Whin - Genista Anglica - Flowers early spring

Bog Myrtle - Sweet Gale - Golden Withy - Myrica Broom

Creeping Willow - Salix repens - Flowers early spring

Ling - Calluna Vulgaris - Flowers August & September.

Heather - Erica Cinerœa - Flowers July & August

Cross-leaved Heather - Erica tetralix - Flowers July & Aug.

Dodder — on Furze beside the road to Robin Hood's Clump

Dwarf red rattle - Honey-Dew - Foxglove Harebell

Bedstraw - Persicaria - Devil's-bit Scabeous - Dock

Mullein - Ragwort - Centaury - Tormentil Burdock

.37.

The Docken's Water & Linwood Bog

List of Plants continued — Marsh Pennywort. Sun-dew
Bog Asphodel. Bog Pimpernel. Cotton-grass. Rush
Figwort. Bog Bean. Pond weed. Sedge-grass
Small sorrel. Early orchis (O. mascula) Spotted orchis. (O.
maculata) Sphagnum (bog moss) mat-grass (Nardus stricta,)
Ground-Ivy. Wild Strawberry. Sloe. Bramble. Braken
Polypody. Iceland Moss. Whortle-berry. Ranunculus hed-
eraceous. Milk-wort. Cuckoo-Flower. Cat-mint. Ladies Tresses
Common Hard Fern. Filix Mas. Myosotis Arvensis. Three
nerved Sandwort. Speedwell. Meadow Thistle. Forget-me-not
Heath-cress. (Teesdalia nudicaulis) Thyme-leaved Veronica. Veronica Agrestis
Fine-leaved Sandwort. Common Veronica. (Officinalis)

.38.

Wild daffies do not grow actually on the common, but close by in Noyce's grounds — near cottage plantation. Orpine grows beside the gulter in Shutler's piece, & below, in further Paradise. The snowdrops that also grow here are probably garden relics. Cow-wheat, also in Shutler's piece. Wood Anemone. Blue Bell. Primrose. Dog-rose. Dog-violet Stitch-wort. Campion. Scarlet Pimpernel. Musk Mallow Bird's Foot Trefoil. Tansy. Self Heal. Succory. Celandine. Red Archangel. Cowslip. Cuckoo-pint. Hairy Bitter-cress. Cow Parsnip Water-Celery. Fumitory. Milfoil. Hoary, & Ribwort Plantain. Cleavers or Goose-grass. Creeping Bugle. Common Tare. Wood-sage. Wood Betony Saw-wort. Blue Flea-bane. St John's Wort. Cud-weed. Common Bird's-foot. Hop Clover.

Boldrewood Farm. 1883

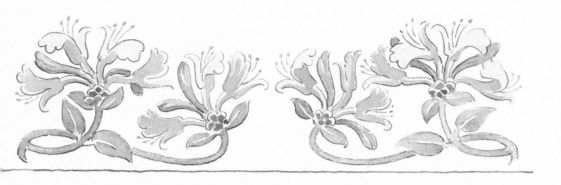

# Cottage Chronicles.

My first visit to the Tame's farm at Boldrewood was
in the year 1882 . Old Tame had been the Duckworth's
gardener at Beechwood, and, at the time I write of,
had retired, & lived with his son & daughter in law,
still however able to do regular garden work, and
occupying a tiny room & a large four post bed.
Indeed granfer's bed was so large that it was used
as a spare room . On occasions, when the farm house
was choke-full, granfer slept at the top of the bed,
& the 3 little grandchildren at the bottom, so he
put in some time as a nursery man as well as in
the garden . He was then an old man, over 80,
shrewd, wise in his garden craft, ready in speech, &
assured in his dissenting self-righteousness . He lived
on into this century, & died at the age of 103 .

In the years 1897 & 1899 I had long talks with the old man, & was impressed by his mental activity. He spent time every day in writing texts on pieces of paper, which he wrapped carefully round smooth stones & gave to the keeper's children to be dropped on the road as they went to Minstead or to Lyndhurst — Someone, he said, would pick up the little parcels, would open them, & read the papers, & just as David overcame Goliath with a sling & 5 smooth stones, so his stones, winged with texts, would surely find their billet.

Old Tame had been a Wesleyan preacher, so his talk was naturally reminiscent of his chapel experience, & the following is a record taken down at the time of some of our conversation when the old man was over 100 years of age.

' My eyesight's garn, can't see 'ee, but I've been reading the bible.' 'Does B. read to you?' ' No ' — with a grave chuckle — 'The Lard reads to me. He called me away from where the men was mowing, when I was 21, beside a girt dog's tomb, & then I knelt down behind that stone & prayed to the Lard. But I kep secret: so I fell away ag & live in sin for 10 years. I was sitting in the church at Bramshaw, in the old sin ful ways, & I was a-looking at the parson, & a-thinking—I shan't get much good out o' 'ee—when the Lord call me the second time, his voice comed out o' the wall "This is no place for 'ee". So I knew I was called for his service, & I comed out o' church, & never been in one since. Yes. I took up with the Wesleyans, & I preached, & so they all took & hated me—"In the world 'ee shall have tribulation"—I knew my enemies would try to overthrow me—They kep say-ing things to my master agen me. One day I was a-praying agen my enemies, by the hot water pipes in the greenhouse, & the Lord heard me, & he took me up from behind, so I knew that I was in the hand of the Lord, & when I come out, my master he comed to me & says—"Jame, I'm a going away for a bit, here's £5 for 'ee to pay the wages, & for to keep 'ee going while I'm away"—And so 'ee see my enemies was all confounded, & so they always have a been.' Then he wandered off into stories of his enemies, how tiresome & wicked they had been, & how continually they had been confounded, so, when I had an opportunity, I tried to change the subject by saying, that I was staying at Bourne-mouth, & had ridden over on my bicycle—'another of the works of the Devil'—So my plan failed!

Another time the old man's talk was of a more serious kind, & I should suppose from the didactic way in which he spoke, that the following was a recollection of one of his chapel sermons — 'Jesus had to be barn of a pure virgin - An 'ooman as know'd nothing. Sarah, nor Elizabeth wouldn't do. Must be a virgin - That was his birth in the speret - Moses & Elijah was the Law - Elijah, he was a law leader, & he looked arter the window of Zarephah - She was a church to 'en, & I've just got to where he rose up her son, but he couldn't raise up the speretual life: but Jesus, he could: he cured the child, & give 'en to his mother.'

Old Tame died in 1900, & his strong character & great age have caused him to be well remembered in all this country side. He was a point of interest in the Forest like one of the most ancient trees — & stories are 'minded' of the old man's sayings & doings — When he was 100, he was dissatisfied with some boots that were made for him at Lyndhurst — they were too thin, so he went to complain, the bootmaker retaliated 'They're thick enough for any walking you'll want', to which he replied 'Well, I've begun my second 100 a good sight stronger than I did my first'—

Old
Tame.

aged 101.
March 1897.

His son — Wᵐ Tame — inherits his Father's power of talking
& is a shrewd story-teller, — here are some of his stories
without their setting, but they were always apposite as he told
them — "That reminds me of a lawsuit about a piece o'land
that was washed out by a flood, the lawyers, they kep on a-
talking about how the land lay afore the flood, & one on
'em calls his witness — What's your name?" — "Adam"—
Where do 'ee live?" — "Paradise" — "How long have 'ee
lived there?" "Afore the flood" — another — "Peter
Warren o' Tharney Down, son o' the smuggler, kep' cattle
& made his living by selling his heifers to butchers at Bourne,
one day he was told that a heifer was suddenly taken ill,
& he had to run home like billy-o' to save his life & cut
his throat — One of Lᵈ Mᵗ Temple's tenants when asked to join in a request for rent reduction, sᵈ he sympathized with 'em, but didden see as how he
cᵈ aske for a reduction, as he hadn't paid any for some years!" —

45.

Old Grant — father of Charles Grant of Royal Oak fame — was a Forest woodman, but had retired from work when I knew him & lived in a little mudwall cottage on Hyde Common beyond Lynch. He is 93 years of age at the date of my writing, thin, deaf, troubled with a cough, but alert in mind & body & with a great mat of white hair, now straight on end, now falling in tufts over his little eyes as he talked — & he was very fond of talking — Here is a story he told me on September 17. 1905. about his father, who painted beautiful.

'    The Queen, she got some paintings by my Father. She told 'en to paint her some game — game. He didden know what game, so he painted a pheasant & 2 partridges & a hare — Beautiful — & then he took em to the Royal Palace — the high Palace, & I went with 'en; & the Queen __was__ pleased, she was terrible took up with 'en — O'course we didden see her, but she paid my Father, & then we went home. Then the Prince he says, he'd like a picture of fish, so my Father went to Tizard at Ibsley & asks 'en if he mid have a fish, & Lard Narmanton tells 'en he mid have any fish he wanted, & so he painted a salmon — Beautiful — & the Prince, he was just as took up as the Queen — So there's two

.46.

pictures painted by my Father a hanging up some-
wheres on the walls of the Royal Palace — the high
Palace.'

The following story was told me by M^rs John Thomas.
Old Grant was at the Royal Oak one day, & the
talk in the bar-room turned upon teeth — & the lack
of them. The old man surprised the talkers by saying
'Well, I never had no teeth, First, nor last'—
'What! You never had no teeth!'— 'Never had
no teeth, first, nor last'— Eventually he explained,
after exciting much curiosity, that First, as a baby,
he had none, & that now, last, he again had none!

Old Grant - aged 94 - July - 1906

On the day in July when I sketched old Grant,
I found his wife was ailing — she was his junior
by 20 years — So I shouted to him that he
must now nurse his wife, instead of her nursing
him. To which he replied — 'So I do, so I do,
I lets her do as she likes' —
'Ah, my stick & me's now full companions, can't
get about without my stick, but its my cough as troubles
me. I used to cough & still feel jockey lar, but it plaggs
me now.' ___
The 'John Thomas' — whom I have mentioned - were my
first friends at Furze Hill. To be precise — Mrs Thomas
was my first friend, for I made her acquaintance when
'Father' was out.        That is now six years ago, &
time has brought about much intimacy. Their cottage
has become a place of friendly resort for all the members
of our household, & a gossip in Mrs Thomas' chimney
corner is part of our life here. She is older than her
husband by 10 years, & sometimes seems old, sometimes
young at 74. 'Oh! Mr Sumner', she would say faintly,
'how are you?' — 'No, I'm terrible rough, its my pore
head, I've such pains all over that I can't set', & then,
after full particulars of all the aches & pains which
wearied her, she would branch off into stories of gaiety,

48.

& courtship, & infants, & midwifery, & death & hardships, prosperity & adversity, in the telling of which her poor head & all-overish pains would be forgotten & the little smoky parlour would be made radiant with reminiscences. She was the daughter of a tailor at Brighton, & had been a cunning needlewoman in her father's business — Waistcoats — Fancy waistcoats — were her special line, & she would tell of how she used to make them for this Duke, & that Nobleman, till it seemed that in the times of forty years ago, the peerage must have been clad by her nimble fingers! Then she had gay memories of dances in her tail-oring days — always was one for dancing — I can mind dancing 32 times round the Assembly rooms at Brighton without stopping — Tales of how her father's health failed; of the disposal of his business; of their retirement to Jersey; of her engagement there to John Thomas, who had come over to see about some early-potatoe venture; of her sudden marriage, (owing to the death of John Thomas' mother,) when she was wanted to keep house at Furzehill, & to help look after the father — And so she married, & lived happily ever after; here; in the same little 3 roomed mud-walled cottage, bringing up 4 boys & 1 girl, (—Lizzie, a deaf mute —) taking care of her invalid

49.

father in-law, doing the housework, & needlework, & dairy-work, & fetching, & carrying. & doing all the endless little jobs that fill the days of a small farmer's wife — Then there would be sometimes tales of illness, — Of The Paralouse — of The Newmonium — of childish ailments '— I can mind when Captain' (the universal nickname for young George Thomas) was abed with Jem along o' the measles, Captain, he always was a terrible one for potaters. always had 'em breakfast, dinner, & tea, well, he got up with measles all over 'en, & crope to the larder, got some cold 'taters, took 'em back to his bed, & keep on eating 'em there. Bimeby Jem he hollers out, 'Mother, the bed ain't comferble, along o' Captain's potaters' — Indeed her stories of cottage sayings & doings were unceasing, & her conver-sation never found wanting. The Thomas' are originally of Welsh extraction, as their name suggests, & are much more emotional than Wessex men are wont to be — more excitable — up & down — with moreover a prompter business vein than most folk possess hereabouts ; & though they have been settled here for 3 generations, & before that, their forefathers lived at Child - Okeford in Blackmore Vale — J.T.69ᵗ 'My granfer he rode up here from Chill Okeford with

50.

my grandmother behind 'en on a pillion, so I've a been
told' — Notwithstanding generations of English upbringing, the Celt survives; Wessex has not subdued Wales.
John Thomas farmed about 40 acres near Furzehill & paid
Lᵈ Normanton £ a year for his small holding. His son
George — Captain — helped him, so did Mrs Thomas, &
did Lizzie; and this family farming is not unusual about
here. The Hayters, The Vineys, The Dundeys, & the
Cohidbornes in a larger way, all carry on farms with fathers
& sons in a sort of labour partnership — Besides this,
the Thomas' did odd jobs, cider making in autumn, hollying
in the winter, gravel carting, ploughing etc for me,
and when first I knew him John Thomas had his
savings invested in a field or two, & in two cottages
at Furzehill. He was a keen, hard-working man,
entirely honourable both in word & deed, & a real good
neighbour. This year — 1907 — illness has interrupted
the joint labour of father & son, and both of them have
been quite disconsolate. Captain has been laid up with
gastric influenza for 3 months, & his recovery of health has been
very halting — 'Captain isn't doing hisself any good. He
just bides at home & studies, & studies, & worrits hisself
a-studying who's a going to do his work; & I tells
'en that his work's got to be done somehow, & so it is,

51.

& would be if he was dead, but he won't cheer up a bit but keeps on studying —" Thus father gives 'Job's comfort' to son.      These two men are fine specimens of modern English countrymen — types of a class that still survive here in spite of half a century of Town made education. Hard of muscle; resourceful; & with habits both of routine & varied work. The management of land, of cattle, of dairy, of horses, of pigs, ploughing, sowing, mowing, threshing, hedging, cider-making, brewing, shooting, all these crafts came in as part of the year's work; while Captain combines these with the skill of a rough Carpenter. Give him an axe, a spade, a hammer & nails, & mark an oak tree — It will be felled, faggoted, chopped into posts, split into pales, & then recreated into as sturdy a pale fence as man can desire. Indeed the everyday ability of such countrymen is my constant admiration, as they ply their varied tasks. —

James Bush — who lives at a lone cottage in the Forest at Woodford Bottom — is a 'super-annivated' forester, chiefly remarkable, I think, for having planted the beautiful yew hedge, which for forty years he has so cunningly tended. To come on such a fine arrangement in such a lonely place, is like finding a rare wild flower that blooms without forethought of admiration — in mere fulfilment of its being.

James Bush's
Cottage at
Woodford
Bottom.

Beyond Woodford Bottom, near High Corner Farm,
is another mud walled lone cottage, so neglected that it
that it seems to be deserted. But it is occupied by Mrs Hatchard,
an old widow; who lives on here quite alone — One day she

53.

gave me her views on politics thus — 'There's two sides so to speak, idden there? Yes, there's the Conservatives, thems for church, & there's the Radicals thems for chapel. No? Well, thats what I've heard tell, & people will keeps talking so till there's no sense left — Now I don't hold altogether with what they Conservatives say, & I don't hold altogether with what they Radicals say, but don't 'ee think the laws want a little altering? — Oh, they women they do go on something shameful. It tidden right — What I say is, the ladies oughter leave the genelmen alone.' —

'What parish is High Carner in? Well its so to speak nowheres — It's what they do call ex-priochal, — ex-priochal, that's what they do call it.'

Mʳˢ Hatchard has lived at this lonely place for 25 years. She thinks that her husband must have died 14 years ago. She used to live at Highwood, 'near the new Sentorium'. (Sanatorium). Should you call, & doubt whether she is at home, you may know that she is out if her wicket latch is bound with holly & brambles. After James Bush's death Decʳ. 1908. she whispered to me — with a furtive dread as to the results — that they 'hadden told the bees' — There is an old belief that when a bee-master dies, the hives should be capped & the bees told, if 'they bees' are to live on. (see. Hardy's short story 'Interlopers at the Knap'. in Wessex Tales.)

James Hayter's Cottage

James Hayter is the representative man of South
Gorley ; by quiet force of character, & by birth
— as a yeoman farmer. Eminently a working stay-
at-home man, & pre-eminently a gentleman.
His farm-cottage, buildings, & garden are his
own, inherited from a line of Hayters who go
back to " I don't know when", and he farms
60 acres of Lord Normanton's land close by,
worked by himself, his son, Tom, Jem Draper,
& Alfred Downer — Father & son can always
be known far away in the fields by their clean

white linen shirts — a fad which both of them affect —
but it is quite vain to advocate flannel, or its substitutes,
when both the linen wearers are sneezing & coughing
in unison, as often happens — They are used to
linen shirts — Mother likes to see 'em — Hard that's
a fact — So there's an end on't !

James Hayter's voice when heard in the
distance, addressing his dog, or his sheep, or a
perverse cow is terrible: it sounds like horrid
imprecations, like cursing & disturbed vitals, it has
a rumbling rasping quality that suggests sin &
the wicked man; but if you brave the terrors of these
of these fearful sounds, & if you meet him, you
find a big, chin-bearded countryman, with a
staid manner, a high voice, & a cackling laugh,
full of wise talk & sensible observation, & cautious
questioning, as is the wont of a real man of Wessex.

Mrs Hayter is a housewife. Hayter is,
as I have said, a stay-at-home man, but compared
to his wife he is a gad-about. Her very
personality deserts her when she is away from home.
She seems to be uprooted & withered — Such times
however are rare, & her being & goodness have
grown by doing her home duties, & by looking after
her immediate neighbours in their troubles.

It shocks her to think of people who live further from a place of worship than she does, (one mile). Yet she is quite tolerant with herself in the matter of chapel-going. Tom, I think, is the most regular of the three, but then he combines it with courting Miss Sine, to whom he has been engaged since 'I can't mind'. But Sunday is a godly day with the Ftayters, a day for special soap scrubbings & shavings, for the whitest of shirts, the stiffest of black silk dresses, for broad-cloth & button-hole flowers, & their cottage & its inmates emanate Sunday in the country unmistakeably. I write with some experience, for every Sunday on our way home from morning church, we stop at the Ftayters & have a gossip, getting cool in summer in their low whitewashed parlour, & warm in winter beside their log-wood fire, & I know that their simple friendliness, & homely life give us something that we shall always remember with affection when we think of Sundays at Cuckoo Ftill.

On week-days, Mrs Ftayter will always be seen bare-armed, girt in a pinned-up skirt & a large over-all apron, with her head-gear chosen from one of Tom's discarded hats – Thus attired she toils at her home-work, her dairy, & her butter-making & selling — and very good butter does she make as we can testify after 4 years of unbroken dealings with her produce –

As to her neigbourly kindness — here is a brief, sad chronicle, as related to me, of last-winter's tale at the Gorley school-house, which shows the quaint & practical character of both James Ftayter & his wife — James Ftayter loq.r —  'Yes, it's very sad, idden it? Poor M.rs Denner; she didden know what she was a-doing; she come running over here, just as we was a going to bed, with never nothing on her feet – just in her night-gown, & she beat on the door & called, so I come down & she was all over trimble, & says Oh what shall I do? I'm sure he's dead – What shall I do? & I says — 'My dear woman get summat on your feet? & then we went over to the school – sure enough Denner was dead.' — M.rs Ftayter loq.r Yes, we was glad to help the poor woman, you see t'was so sudden, & M.rs Denner she wasn't partial to corpses, so I laid 'en out myself, & I must say he made a very pleasant corpse'. 'Yes' said James Ftayter 'Denner made a pleasant corpse' –

'The Friendly Society at Goreley', established

58.

in 1810, used to hold its meetings in 'the club-room' at the Hayter's cottage — A triple-locked box containing their account book, (1846 to 1871) & rules, still remains among the various lumber of the old house — as also the banner carried at the 50th anniversary of the Society in 1860. The rules show that a member paid 2/6 entrance fee, (raised to 5/ in 1860) & $4^s$ quarterly — In case of illness a member received 6/a week for the first 6 weeks of his illness, & 3/a week after then. £2 was paid on death, every member had to attend the funeral, & had to contribute 1/ to the member's widow or representative.

The following items are of curious interest —
1846. 'John Cutler died June $2^{nd}$ owen been Cick by a hors?
1848. 'Received of $W^m$ Hayter one year's Intress due Midsummer Qurter for the youse of 10 pounds'
1848. 'Memorandem that Job Hayter was fined for resley we Charles Plumbley gone home on Monday the Qurter night, & in falen Brocke his lag, Fine, $5/^o$ —
1849. 'Chas. Thomas Finde for Baten out the Canales on Midsummer Qurter night before he went away. fine, $2/6^o$ — * see appendix. p. 176.

On the Jubilee day of the Society, July 21, 1860, there were 105 members on the roll. The feast expenses came to £8.16-9. (the item £3.11.2. malt & hops, suggests home brew.) 2ˢ was the charge for the feast, ahead, (2/6 now,) — The doctor received 2/6 a year for each member — — In 1851. an entry shows labour was paid 1ˢ 2ᵈ a day — — The names of members, even in the oldest roll in the book (1846), sound familiar, & testify to the continuity of country families in their place — Philpott. Pope, Flayter, Holloway. Dear. Parker. Cutler. Goff. Head. Curtis. Shutler. Thomas. Noyce. Dymott. Brown. Sinsbury. Downer. Marlow. Grant. Bason. Witt. Gibbs. Deaken. Seiver. Sandy — all well known names here to this day.

— The Honorary members are entered as 'Honnored Members', or 'Honned Members', in 1846 they were. * The Rev. Chas Hatch. The Rev Mʳ Green, Mʳ Arthur Venable. Mʳ Henry Venable. Mʳ Arthur Paset. Mʳ Alx Carter. Mʳ Westcoatt. Mʳ Stephen Coals — & contributed £4.2ˢ.6ᵈ In succeeding years other 'Honnored members' join. The Rev Mʳ Hamon. Leady Venable, Mʳ White Flayter, Mʳ Hutton the butcher. Mʳ Chas. Ingram. The Rᵛ Mʳ Bartlett — 'The Leady Venable to sons'. I take to be Mʳ Arthur & Henry Venable 'Mʳ Westcoatt' sometimes is entered as 'Mʳ Weskett' he has 'surgeon' after his name in the entry of 1851. The Rᵛ

H.C Warren, Mr Chas Thomas, Mr Wm Read, The Rd E. Bankes
The Rd Hamilton Davis & S.S. Dyer Esqrs are names
that appear as Honorary members in more recent years.
The last entry in the account book from which I have
been quoting is dated Lady day 1871, at which date
the Society numbered 52 members, I believe that
shortly afterwards it came to an end — The present
Gorley Slate Club was founded about 25 years ago
on the relics of the old "Friendly Society at Gorley"
but without direct succession ——

Hatch was vicar of Fordingbridge & Everett his curate, both were Cambridge men, & had
mutual friends there : by ill·luck, one of these friends gave both of them a Cambridge
sermon that had been held worthy of print. One Sunday morning, when Everett was
officiating at Ibsley, Hatch preached this excellent sermon at Fordingbridge. G. Rawlence,
one of the churchwardens, fully endorsed the Cambridge verdict "The best sermon I ever
heard the vicar preach". In the evening, Everett preached, Hatch having read the
service, & being seated in the reading desk, under the pulpit. Then he heard his
morning text, followed by his morning sermon! During the ordeal, he is said to have
gradually sunk from view in his seat behind the reading desk : and when he met
his churchwarden with apology & explanation, he cannot have been
quite gratified on being told by G. Rawlence "Well we never supposed
that all your sermons were your own, & we laity are glad to have
a double·dose of a good thing" — (Told me by Elias Squarey of
the Moot Downton.)

61.

Blunt's Barn Cottage

Blunt's Barn cottage was begun in Oct.ʳ 1905. I em-
ployed 2 bricklayers & 2 labourers for the job, while
Alexander supplied lime, cement, scaffold, woodwork
& Carpenters, adding 10% to the cost of material &
time. The bricks came from Blissford, at 32/ a 1000
— 1ˢ. 6ᵈ less than supplied for the house, in consideration
of the cottage being at the bottom of the hill — The
whole job, including well, post & rail fence, wicket &
lean-to pig-stye, gravel paths etc, came to £233:
but some saving was made on the staircase, which
was removed from the garden passage at Cuckoo
Hill — The items will be found on p. 4. of my Farm

63.

Hungerford Lynch.

& garden cash book . This cottage is let to Harry Roberts
at 3/6 a week — £9.2 a year —
The cottage that I designed for Champion Russell at Hungerford Lynch was built by Alexander . His contract was
£275: but there were various extras — such as a 1300
gallon rain water tank — Ballam's tiles instead of Bridgewater, etc, & when it was finished it came to £346.
The estimate for the stable & barn was £158, & they
cost £177. with extras of which the principal were
rain-water drain, torching the Bridgewater tiles, &
cementing the inside walls of the barn.
I think that this cottage is an improvement on mine.
Specially in the double lean to at the back — see plan p.65.
& in the ground floor windows being 5 panes high instead
of 4 panes . Here, where bricks are fairly good & handy
you cannot do better than 12". hollow brick wall, roughcasted

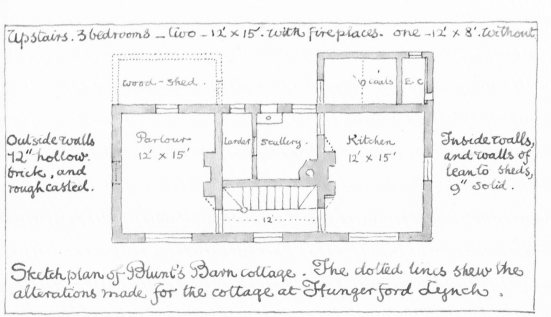

Upstairs. 3 bedrooms — two — 12' x 15'. with fireplaces. one — 12' x 8'. without

wood - shed.

coals    E.C

Outside walls
12" hollow.
brick, and
rough casted.

Parlour
12' x 15'

larder  scullery.

Kitchen
12' x 15'

Inside walls,
and walls of
lean-to sheds,
9" solid.

12

Sketch plan of Blunt's Barn cottage. The dotted lines shew the
alterations made for the cottage at Hungerford Lynch.

The old method of mud-walling — puddled clay & rushes — is
excellent, when it is well done, but the chances are against
good work. For this reason. The wall is raised — like concrete
in boarded 'rearings'; 1 foot 6 in: at a 'rearing'. Four men meet,
puddle, & raise a 'rearing', then they leave the job for a fortnight
while it dries — They meet again; & if there has been drying
weather meantime, the next 'rearing' goes up on a firm lower
course: not so however if there has been broken weather, yet
in such an event the temptation is great for men who have met
by arrangement to put in a day's work — probably they go
on with the next 'rearing', & the result is a weak wall that
'bags' with the weight which it is not ready to bear. And
this is the cause of most of the failures in mud-walling.
There is very little mud-walling done now here-abouts,
& the craft is dying out.

65.

Calluna Vulgaris —          Erica Tetralix —          Erica Cinerea

## Heath Fires.

For the first 3 years of our life at Cuckoo Hill we were undisturbed by heath fires on Ibsley Common. Occasionally furze bushes were set alight on Gorley Hill, but they only made a grand blaze, & after creating mild excitement, died down leaving but a small blackened patch in the morning as record of what seemed to be a great fire on the preceding night. Fires also we had seen every Spring far up in the Forest, or across the valley on the Plumley, Verwood, & S^t Ives heath lands; some authorised burnings, such as the great furze fire on Latchmoor on Easter Monday 1905, some unauthorised — by accident, on purpose —; but never had the fires come near us, nor did we know the dangerous speed of a heath fire running before the wind, till the spring of 1906 when Ibsley common was burnt across from

end to end — From the top of Brogenslade to Newlands —
and this is how it came about.

Furze-hill was the starting point. Furze-hill is rightly
named, & of late years the commoners were complaining
that the Furze had made too much growth. It was
encroaching on the Feed. Accordingly I drew up a
petition to Lord Normanton, the Lord of the Manor
thus.        To. E. P. Scholfield. Esqre        — March 12 1900

        Sir. We, the undersigned commoners of
Ibsley Common, should be very much obliged if you would
bring the following request before Lord Normanton —
namely, That we should be allowed to burn the Furze
& heath on the part marked red, (Brogenslade & Leaden
-hall) on the enclosed sketch plan of the Common.

Of late years the Furze has very much increased, con-
-sequently the feed has diminished, & the danger of
unauthorized fires has increased. We believe that
such authorized burning as we are now venturing to
propose to his Lordship would be of great benefit to the
Feed, & of no damage to the sporting value of the
Common, as the portion we indicate is not frequented
by game.        If, as we hope, his Lordship will favour-
-ably consider our request, we would all undertake
to assist in the burning, & keep it within bounds,
& would fulfill to the best of our ability all such

68.

conditions as it may be thought fit to impose — signed Heywood Sumner, John Thomas _ James Hayter. James Viney Stephen Shutter. George Thomas _ James Thomas. Charles Pope _ G. Wickham _ Wyatt _ Alfred Bundy _ Samuel Philpott _ Henry Bason . T. F. C. Reed _ James Banks.

In due time we got the following reply —

Gentlemen                                                    March 22. 1906

I now write to say that I have seen Lord Normanton with reference to your letter of the 12th inst: & your request as to the burning of certain portions of furze & heath on Ibsley Common.

Lord Normanton is very willing that you should carry out what you suggest provided every care is taken to keep the burning within proper bounds, & that he is not held responsible for any damage to property. I feel sure that every care will be taken — Believe me, gentlemen,

your obedient servant . E. P. Scholfield

So that was all right. Accordingly, we arranged a convenient day, & on Saturday, March 31. we all assembled at 9 o'clock in the morning, & with solemn publicity began to set fire to the furze patches along the Huckles brook . They behaved just like the furze fires on Gorley Hill, the flames blazed up furiously, & then abruptly died down without any attempt at spreading . And so each man went about with burning furze brands setting light

69.

to the straggling patches. Furze-hill soon was smoking with in-numerable fires. Toomen with their babies stood watching on the lew side; the children were scared by the crackle & roar of the flames, & really behaved with remarkable caution; while Lizzie Thomas made strange inarticulate sounds of warning whenever the fires seemed dangerously near to their fernrick.

From Furze-hill we burnt our fiery way up ~ Brogenslade, & all went well till we got to the deep rutted drokes at top: here the furze-brakes are thickly fringed with heather & long sage grass; & here we found to our cost that we had lit more fires than we could control. A brisk North Wester too sprang up. & the fire began running, across the droke, up the hill, & away over the plain: followed by a fringe of beaters: about ten of us; & by dint of persistent beating with fir-boughs we succeeded in keeping the running fire within some bounds, but failed to stop it till it reached Ladywell; & here, at the deep droke leading to North Hollow bridge, we finally beat out the fire.

By 3 o'clock we could safely leave the charred ground & although we had burnt more than we intended to burn, still no real damage had been done. So far, so good, & when on our way home John Thomas met us in Brogenslade with a can of welcome cider, to

we could slake our thirsty, smoke-dried throats, &
feel well pleased at the success of the first authorised
burning of the Common within the memory of man.

Our pleasure was short-lived. At night unauthi
orised fires sprang up, first in several places on Gorley
& then beyond Mockbeggar. The latter was a very
big blaze, for the furze & heath had grown high on the
southerly lew of the hills, & this fire raged furiously
from 9 o'clock to the small hours of Sunday morning.
The wind was high & was blowing more westerly
than in the morning, & Newlands was only saved
from the flames by timely back-burning directed
by Gallie. (the estate woodman) The result of this fire
was that all the hills between Mockbeggar & Newlands,
and a large piece of Whitefield plain were burnt to
a cinder-ground. The turf cutters grumbled at the
loss of a specially good turf-ground, while the
keepers — wholly disclaiming the fire — approved the result,
as it would save them trouble in looking for outlying
pheasants' nests.

Then followed a week of warnings & nightly
watchings. On Monday morning I heard indirectly
that 'they' meant to burn the furze on Cuckoo Hill,
& in the afternoon, as I was bicycling to Stuckton to
tell Harfield — the policeman — to be on the look out, I

71.

was stopped by Marlow's up-raised arm. Again the same warning. "'They' were going to burn Cuckoo's Hill tonight". Accordingly the policeman in plain clothes Philpott, Harry & I lurked about on the hill until 11. o'clock in the hope of catching 'They'. But in vain. Distant fires at Godshill, & beyond Picked Post lighted up the horizon, & kept us on the alert, & from time to time we caught each other after elaborate stalking among the furze brake; but the threat of which I had been warned was not fulfilled —

Throughout the week we continued on the watch & on most nights there were fires either on Gorley Hill, Rockford Common, Linwood bog or across the valley at Plumley. On Sunday night we expected a respite — out of respect to Sunday clothes, if not to the day! but Blackmore interrupted our Sunday supper by the unwelcome news of a great fire on the common. Sure enough it was a great fire that we saw as soon as Michael & I went out of the back door. The rounded hills above Shutter's Cottage were fringed with running flames. Rings of fire were creeping round the Eastern sides of Dorridge. While spouts of fire, sparks, & dense smoke behind Dorridge clumps, shewed that the self sown thickets of little firs had been lighted on the Western side.

72.

Michael ran up to the fire, armed with a fir-tree beater – of which I had now laid in a stock – while I kept guard on our hill, as, with fires about, I feared more might happen & nearer home. He was the first at the fire that was now burning up on the plain beyond North Hollow gravel-pit, & I soon heard his halloos for help, which were presently answered from Furze Hill. Then Philpott came along the top of Cuckoo Hill where I was watching, & so I left him in charge, with Harry, who had also appeared, & went up myself to the fire-beating line.

There was a high North-west wind blowing, & the fire had become quite unmanageable. It was difficult to maintain effective beating owing to the gusty wind, & the heat of the driven flames that rushed up & down the hills with a sinister flapping roar; while fiery clouds of racing smoke magnified the fire to vast proportions. A few men with fir-boughs seemed very puny opposition to such a raging element. At first we feared for Robin Hood's clump, – from which in passing we had helped ourselves to fir boughs – and that the fire would come along our hill, but we managed by vigorous beating to keep it above the top end of Great Chibden bottom, & turned it before it reached Newtown; while on the further side of the common the fire

73.

just skirting the western end of Whitefield clump, fin-
-ally burnt itself out on the plain above Dockbeggar, on the
previous burning of the week before. After we had passed
Chibden bottom — where the fire was specially fierce — it
was possible for our line of 8 or 10 men to beat out the
flames as fast as we could walk, as soon as we got
on to places where turf cutting had left bare patches;
& so, after three hours of incessant beating, & beating,
with blistered hands, & with our boughs worn bare, &
burnt with our job, the fire was out: At one o'clock on
Monday morning we left the Common in darkness.

A strange incident of these fires on Ibsley common
was the running accompaniment of explosions that here
& there followed the flames . They were caused by
Soldier's cartridges which had been dropped during the
manœuvres of 1898, & that were now at last discovered
by the searching fire , & tested after years of exposure
in the moss & heather . Certainly we may claim that
we keep our powder dry.

Two young men from 'ups along', Wilt & Goudge
by name , were caught lighting furze on Gorley Hill, &
they got 2 months apiece for thus misusing a matchbox;
but the fires on Ibsley Common kept their own secret,
their lighting up was never traced, & remains a matter of dark
suspicion, of hints , & of solemn knowing nods among evil-

74.

Robin Hood's clump

informed heads.

The Common quickly recovered from its blackened state. In three week's time, green blades were pushing up through the ashes, & the ponies & the sheep were nibbling the tender tops of the young sage grass. By June the heather had begun to shoot, & the burnt furze to break from the roots, surrounded by innumerable seedlings, while the fern had run riot all over Brogenslade, across Great Chibden bottom on to Whitefield plain. Indeed these parts of the Common were much greener than heretofore; but — apart from fern — the hills by Newlands & Mockbeggar still (July) retain their charred desolation.

Burn the bottoms, but not the hills is the lesson taught by these fires, & moreover, burn Early in the year. The importance of burning early was shewn on the hills near Ladywell, for here, on the Ogdens purlieu side, there was a fire in May or June 1905, &, with the exception of scanty fern growing in the hollows, these grounds remain bare & brown. Now, the part that we burned in March 1906 has much more growth on it in three months, than the other has in thirteen months.

The charred stems of the furze bushes are perhaps the ugliest relics of heath fires. They remain tough & stand for a year, when they rot at the root, & are then broken off either by children for firewood, or by the wandering cattle.

During August & September all three kinds of heath made strong growth, & came into late flower. The dwarf gorse also flowered throughout the autumn.

Neither ponies, cows, nor sheep seemed to nibble over these young growths, till the autumn, when I noticed cows & heifers cropping the tops of the young ling, & in the winter, they preferred this feed to any other part of the common.

Note. Heather burning is controlled in Scotland by an Act passed in 1773 whereby any person setting fire to heath or moor between April 11. & Nov. 1. is on conviction liable to a penalty of £2 for for the first offence. £5. for the second, & £10 for the third, & every subsequent offence, or, failing payment, imprisonment. 'The keeper's Book' by Walker & Mackie.

76.

White field – after the fire

In February 1907 the moss-tufts — which I thought had been quite killed by the fires — began to recover, & to show a tinge of green on top of their dead grey tussocks. The sturdy growth of the dwarf gorse was shewn in the same month when Powell's beagles were hunting hares — of which there were too many — on the common : then, if they had not a hare before them, they soon lost heart for their job of ranging over the creeping growth of prickles, & gave up trying.    We had a pretty sight on that day On the plain, just beyond Leadenhall, a beautiful fox got up, close to me, from a snug form in the dry iceland moss & heather, & his fur shone ruddy far across the plain as he dodged & jumped over the dark heath on his open road to Hasley.

In 1907, E. P. Scholfield sent round the following notice to the Commoners, "A Meeting will be held at Gorley School, on Friday, the 12th of April, at 7.30. p.m. which all those who have Common rights on Gorley, Ibsley, & Rockford Commons are invited to attend, to discuss the question of systematic burning of the heather on these Commons so as to prevent, if possible, incendiary Fires". It was a pouring wet evening when we met – The elements evidently were blessing our endeavours to prevent incendiary fires! About 30 Commoners attended – Scholfield took the chair, expressed Ld Normanton's interest in the matter, & asked for the opinion of those present as to the best way of organizing yearly burnings on the commons. James Hayter, John Thomas, Viney, Roberts, & I contributed to the discussion, – It was generally agreed that heath & furze burning in selected patches would be a great benefit – That it was now too late for heath burning, & indeed, that there was no burning needed on either Ibsley or Rockford Commons after the great fires of last year; but that a specified belt of furze should be burned as soon as possible on Gorley Common Eventually I moved & James Hayter seconded a resolution to this effect – " It is agreed by this meeting of Gorley, Ibsley, & Rockford Commoners,

Linwood bog

that there shall be an annual meeting of the said
Commoners in the month of February to arrange
for such burning as may be necessary, & other
matters connected with the Commons' — This
was carried unanimously, & the meeting dispersed
at 8.30 after a vote of thanks to Schofield
proposed by Thomas, seconded by Wickham.
        On Friday, April 19, we had an authorised
burning of the piece of furze on Gorley Common; from
the top of Puddles to Deacon's cottage, thence up to
'racecourse' path, then across to the top of the gravel
pit . It was a still day, & the furze burned well, but
needed much lighting owing to its patchy growth.
We began at 10 o'clock & finished at 4. o'clock.
The result can now (August) be judged, & the feed
on the burnt part is much improved.

On Monday, March 16, 1908 we had another authorised burning on Ibsley Common — after a preliminary meeting in February at the school which was largely attended by commoners of Ibsley, Gorley & Rockford. In the morning we burnt from the top end of Chibden bottom, across the plain at Leaden-hall, & down the far side hills to Linwood bog, thus dividing the common by a broad track of burnt ground, so that a fire cannot now run from end to end of the Common — as it did two years ago.

— Alas for ingenuity! my cherished hope of a Roman place-name derivation for Leaden-hall. (see p. 31) was destroyed today by Stephen Shutler* the Furze hill turf cutter — "Why was this called Leaden-hall? well the plain here is terrible poor, & when you do cut turves they turns up sorter lead colour, as you mid say, not brown, like they turns up in the bottoms, & that's why they do call it Leaden-hall." — Alas, for Leden or Roman Hill!

In the afternoon we burnt large tracts on both sides of Chibden bottom. Throughout the day the fires burnt well, & never got out of hand — We put up 3 hares on Leadenhall plain; and a hunted buck crossed the common, coming from Newlands & going to Broomy. There was no scent when the hounds came to the burnt ground which the buck had crossed.

By the end of May the burnt furze in Chibden was shooting at the roots, & hundreds of seedlings were showing. The fern was a foot high & the sedge grass abundant — The old furze suffered greatly from the snow fall in April, & must be burnt next year.

80.

Piece of Heath to be burnt.

Direction of wind

Light here after the stop track fires 1.2.3.4 have been beaten out

Keep the fire within bounds at 5.5.-5.5.

How to keep a heath <u>Fire in hand</u> — Burn a stop track at the down wind end of the piece of heath that is meant to be burnt — Thus — First, light fires at 1. 2. 3 & 4. Sufficiently near to intersect each other when they have burnt a small fiery circle — thus they will burn themselves out, except at the outsides, which must be beaten out — Do not light more of these track fires than your beaters can manage. When the stop track has been thus burnt & beaten out ; Set alight to the up wind end of the main piece of heath to be burnt, which can be kept under at the sides, & will burn itself out when it comes to the already burnt stop track.

* Stephen Shutler when speaking of having been surprised, says, "I was took non-plush".

81.

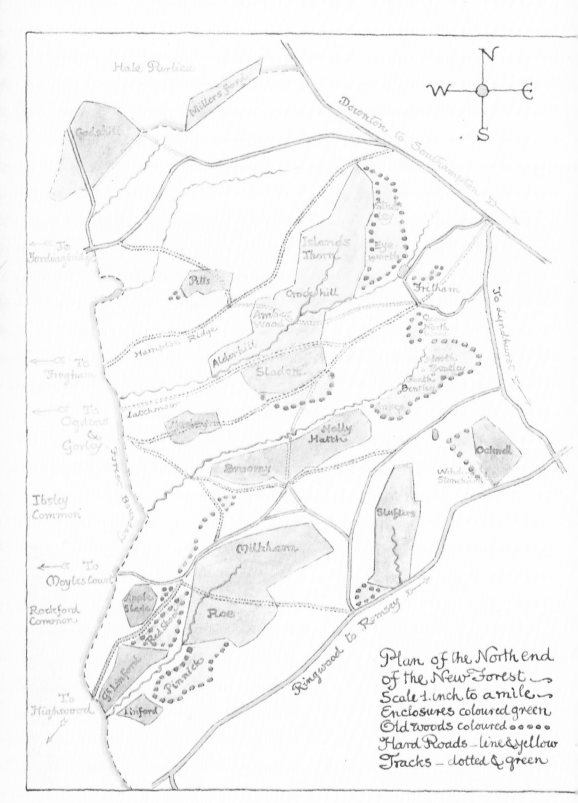

N

W     E

S

Hale Purlieu

Millers Ford

Godshill

*Downton to Southampton*

Studley

Islands Thorn

Eye worth

To Fordingbridge

Pitts

Crockhill

Fritham

Queen North Wood

Amber Wood

Alderhill

North Bentley South Bentley

To Frogham

Hampton Ridge

Sladen

To Sandhurst

Anses

Latchmoor

Hasley

Holly Hatch

Ocknell

To Ogdens & Gorley

Windley Stonecross

Broomy

Ibsley Common

Slufters

Forest Boundary

To Moyles Court

Milkham

Rockford Common

Apple Slade

Roe

Ringwood to Romsey

Gt Linford

Pinnick

To Highwood

Linford

Plan of the North end
of the New Forest
Scale 1 inch to a mile
Enclosures coloured green
Old woods coloured ○ ○ ○ ○
Hard Roads — line & yellow
Tracks — dotted & green

82.

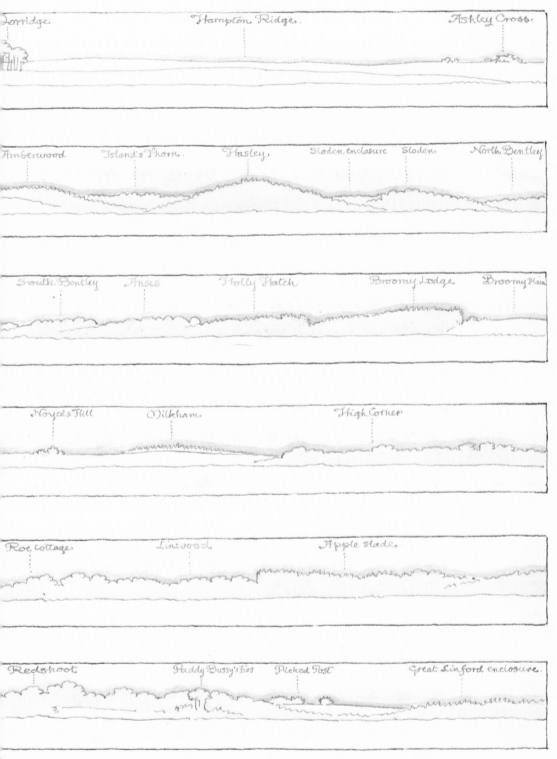

Dorridge.      Hampton Ridge.      Ashley Cross.

Amberwood   Island's Thorn.   Hasley.   Sloden enclosure   Sloden.   North Bentley

South Bentley   Anses   Holly Hatch   Broomy Lodge.   Broomy Plain

Noyce's Hill   Milkham.   High Corner

Roe cottage.   Linwood   Apple slade.

Redshoot   Paddy Bussy's ties   Picked Post   Great Linford enclosure.

Outline of the Forest horizon as seen from Robin Hood's Clumps. (left to right)

Looking West from Ocknell Plain.

# The Forest

The Forest suggests trees; green tracks through inter-
minable trees; no clear sky; but above, waving branches,
below, tree trunks & tangle; shadowy gloom as the
trees descend the valleys, & a broken vision of multitudinous
tree-tops on wooded hills. Up & down, trees, trees,
innumerable trees.

But this does not describe our side of the Forest.
Here, on the Northern side — and the Ringwood &
Romsey road may be taken as the boundary between the
North & South sides of the Forest — here, we have
long rolling hills of heather, fern, & furze, worn into

five parallel ridges & furrows by streams that trickle in dry, & rush in wet weather down gravelly courses to the broad valley of the Avon – Here & there are thickets of holly, thorn, yew & crab-apple – Here & there are old woods of oak, beech, yew, holly, thorn & white beam. Here & there are enclosures of Scots fir, oak & sweet chesnut. But the main features of our side of the New Forest are, heather uplands, winding moorland streams, & scattered woods. The open country is never far distant. Afoot or a-wheel you may learn the same thing. The tracks from Highwood, & Ogdens & Frogham to Fritham, and the roads from Ringwood & Fordingbridge & Downton to Cadenham, all give far views over wild foregrounds to distant cultivation: They reveal the vision of a primæval waste, set in the midst of an older and more fertile formation; of heath-lands surrounded by the chalk hills of Dorset, Wilts, Hants, & the Isle of Wight; and they tell that the Bag-shot Beds, on which you stand, are deposited over a great trough of chalk that dips from Badbury & Pent ridge to the Island, and from Purbeck to the Hamp-shire South Downs.

'Live on land, but praise the sea,' says the old proverb – 'Live on gravel, but praise the chalk,' is a

86.

ater version in my Book of Wisdom.

I was born & bred on Hampshire chalk, & love it, — but — I do not love it as a home when the rains fall and the springs rise in the New Year — Then, during the months of January, February, & March, the chalk-white bosom of old Mother Earth is deadly cold; wet through & through; and the usual, keen air, instead of being laden with infinite scents from miles of flowery downlands, has a clammy breath, & chills to the very marrow.

And here, our coldest winds in the early year come from the great chalk uplands of Cranborne Chase which bound our distant view in the West & North West. But we escape the ground cold of that soil. The winds may be keen, but they do not search rheumatic bones; and for the rest of the year they bring us that fine quality of air that seems to be specially distilled by the chalk as the breezes pass over its ancient coat of sheep-trimmed turf.

Thus we live on gravel & praise the chalk, and our Benedicite is shared by all the Forest Cattle; they know where the winds blow refreshment, & their summer shades are up on the plains, above the sluggish air of the shut-in valleys; on Godshill & Telegraph hill, at Longcross & Ocknell, at Handycross & Broomy, the ponies & foals & tinkling cows stand through the hot summer days, cooled by the breeze

Sloden Hill.

that comes over sea or chalk-land ; and so, like us, they
also praise the distant hills by their choice.

Now in this chapter, I should like to be able to give some
sort of record of the present life & look of this Northern end of the
Forest. Something that will enable my reader of A.D. 2000.
to see, as I now see, these wild hills & woods & valleys — a
vision that Time, & the changes & chances will otherwise surely
relegate to the dark limbo of vanished Forest life. And with
this end in view, I think that pages of pictures will be more
illuminating than pages of writing. How much I should like

Ragged Boys Hill.

to see drawings of old Sloden hill before the enclosure was made in 1864. Or Hasley hill before it was enclosed & planted in 1846. Or Godshill when, as Lewis tells, it was covered with pollards, & so much holly was growing upon it that a person might mistake his road'. Accordingly I shall attempt to do for others, as I would they had done for me. I shall trust to my pencil rather than to my pen. I shall tell the unborn reader whom I serve, that there are three indispensable books dealing, from different points of view, with the New Forest — namely — Lewis' Topographical remarks on the ancient & modern state of the New Forest. published

89.

The track from Sloden to Latchmoor

in 1811. Gilpin's remarks on Forest Scenery, edited by Sir Thomas Dick Lauder. published 1834. and Wise's, The New Forest, its history & scenery . published 1862 (several editions since) & that the article on Forestry & the New Forest, by Nisbet & Lascelles in the 2nd volume of The Victoria History of Hampshire. publish 1903 is a real contribution to the literature on this subject: and I shall content myself with supplementing these authors by adding minor local details concerning things that were outside the scope of their learned enquiries .

As we grow older, there arises a new interest in such local facts, coupled with a certain impatience toward romantic

admiration that is satisfied with inaccuracy; and it is this mediæval state of mind, & this sphere of curiosity that will be evident in the following pages. Accordingly, in pursuance of this plan, I begin with a list of & with notes on the present woods & enclosures on the Northern side of the Forest — The various dates of the Enclosures are taken from the map appended to the Return relating to the New Forest Ap. 15. 1875.

Alder-hill. planted in 1869. still enclosed. Scots fir & oak: some old yews, & alders, that give the reason of the name, are buried in the young plantation. Dog-wood bushes

Hampton Ridge

grow in the thickets on Latchmoor just below Alder hill
both alder & dogwood were used for gun-powder making
when the industry was first started at Eyeworth.
Boletus luridus grows in the rides - If cut in two, the section
from white turns to a dull blue - poisonous. Fly Agarics come
up every year, just outside the enclosure where the green
track to Fritham emerges on Latchmoor - poisonous. This track
is a great place for fungi - Boletus edulis, chantarelles (edible
Agaricus dealbatus, Russulas. Clavaria Vermiculata. H. Coccineus

Latchmoor

<u>Amberwood</u>. planted in 1815. mostly oak with undergrowth of blackthorn & fern. at the top there is a belt of fine Scots fir & Weymouth pine, under which grow whortleberry plants but without berries*. I have seen a herd of 15 buck in this wood. On Cockly plain, in 1903, I came across three black cock dusting themselves in the road — not far from Deadman's Hill. Since then, we have never put up black grouse in our many Forest walks. James Bush tells that in years gone by, they

*They grow thus, on the high grounds, throughout this side of the Forest

93.

South Bentley

were plentiful on this side of the Forest, & that he can mind their 'curling' on the hills round Sloden.

Anses. old beech, oak, holly & crab-apple. The beeches in this wood are the most beautiful old trees on this side of the Forest. Butcher's Broom grows at the top end. Fly Agarics at the lower end.

AppleSlade. planted in 1829 – oak, scots fir, & sweet chestnut. in some years the last ripen their mast, & we go gathering nuts

Anses.

in October: hydnum repandum, edible, grows beside
the top rides. Agaricus Æruginosus — verdigris mushroom —
outside, near Redshoot.

<u>Broomy</u>. planted in 1809. mostly oak with fern under-
growth. Our fern litter comes from here, or from Appleslade,
or from Roe. 8ˢ a waggon-load, paid to the woodman,
who cuts & pooks the fern, ready for removal. Between
Broomy & High Corner, on Noyce's hill, club moss, also
called stag's horn moss, grows in large patches. Bogbean

is plentiful beside the brook. Curlews nest in the bogs between Broomy & Hasley — And now, O reader of another century Forbear — Remember the Rime of the Ancient Mariner, the curse that fell on him, & his lamentable penance. I cannot tell whether a curlew shot by a gun, would have baneful

Palmer's Slough

...ower, as had the harmless Albatross, shot by the Mariner's cruel bow; but at least I, who tell you where wild things live & grow, may demand a promise — namely — that you will not mis-use my Telling, & that you will not dis-possess these freeholders of the Forest whose claim is older than that

Ticketsbury & Pitts wood

of the Grown .          Indeed you may find far more pleasure
in watching the yearly return of this or that bird or beast
to the same haunt, or the yearly upgrowth of rare wild
plants that stubbornly occupy their holding against en
-croachment — far more pleasure, than in pointing to a glass
case, & a stuffed bird, with the mention of hills where now
do curlews cry, or than in spoiling the garden of Pan for
sake of a few wild flowers in a vase . Please forbear —
Remember — 'I wandered lonely as a cloud', — Before it

Hive Garn Bottom

was Coleridge, now it is Wordsworth ― Remember the host
of daffies dancing by the lake, & the abiding vision of his
inward eye ― and know that is only vouchsafed to such
as keep their hands from picking & stealing, & to those who
love the green things, even to leaving them in their wild estate ―
Note ― Club-moss also grows by some old yews, near a gate leading into
Sloden Enclosure, at the top of Watergreen Bottom. On April 15, 1907
Humphrey & I heard & saw a pair of curlews at Hallicks Hole. But
they did not nest here ― Club-moss grows outside Broomy. W. side, near a chestnut.

99.

Splash bridge — Near Holly Hatch.

<u>Eyeworth</u> — old beech & holly. Individually, these old beeches are not specially fine, but their mossy trunks rising out of the holly undergrowth, which covers the hill, give a distinct char--acter to this wood.

<u>Godshill</u>. planted in 1810 — oak & scots fir. outside the wood on the East, broomrape grows among the furze near the road. (Godshill, probably a pagan site consecrated to Christian worship — Isaac Taylor.)

Holly Hatch. Lilies of the valley grow at the top end of the wood,
eft, coming up the main ride leading to Ocknell Plain.

Hasley) planted in 1846 — still enclosed - Scots fir, larch, oak
& sweet chestnut - Just outside the enclosure, on the North,
& again on the North East, the sandy soil is of a deep orange
colour, & full a curious iron stone formation called limonite -
Broad, the woodman at Amberwood, told me that he once
used some of this sand in his chicken-run with the result

Greenford Bottom & Pinnick

that the white fowls were stained rusty yellow. I have
often seen deer & foxes in this enclosure.
Holly Hatch — planted in 1808. oak & Scots Fir, with thick
thorn & holly undergrowth. (Hatch — a hitch-gate, a common
suffix in the neighbourhood of ancient forests _ Isaac Taylor _)

102.

Great Linford. planted in 1846 _ still enclosed _ oak & Scots
fir . Columbines are occasionally to be found by the stream outside
the enclosure. also wild daffies . by the stream, & within
the enclosure, at the Northern corner.

103.

Redshoot.

Linford enclosure . planted in 1846

Note. Picked Post, on the high plain above Linford enclosure
is spelt thus in Lewis' map of the Forest, but Picket in modern
maps . Picked = pointed . it was not a marking stake name
but perhaps a sign-post name. Again Picket Corner, at the top end
of Studley wood, marks a place where the wood ends in a point of a wedge .
i, e, Picked, or pointed.

Island's Thorn & Crock Hill planted in 18
These names distinguish different parts of one large enclosure

n Crock Hill are remains of British pottery works, (see
rise's New Forest, & Victoria history of Hampshire,) Panshard
till near Amberwood is a place name with the same origin
s Crock Hill. I have found shards & crocks of this ancient
ottery outside newly dug rabbit holes on the site of the works.
A favourite haunt of deer. I have seen a herd of 14 just outside
e enclosure.

Dilkham - planted in 1861. still enclosed. Scots Fir a haunt
f red deer.

<u>Pinnick</u>. an old wood of stunted oak & thorn growing on ver stiff clay. The name Pinnick is probably connected with some forester. There are many families of this name hereabouts. At Ridle wood – just over the hill. & across the high road, you may find clusters of Agaricus adiposus on the roots of the beeches, & Agaricus mucidus, gleaming white & shiny on the mossy boughs of the oldest trees.

<u>Pitt's Wood</u>. planted in·· 5. fine oaks & holly. Butcher Broom grows near Ashley Lodge. This wood was re-enclosed in 1904. partly replanted in 1905. & a nursery for young trees made at the Tickets-bury end of the wood.

<u>Queen North Wood</u>. old oak. Beech, & holly.

<u>Red Shoot</u>. a beautiful old wood of oak. holly, crab apple & yew, on a clay hill. 'Shoot' is – hill – & it may be called Red because of the colour of the soil. A favourite haunt of deer Butterfly orchises grow in plenty among the heather glades –

<u>Roe</u>. planted in 1811. I have seen red deer rutting here. Columbines grow at the lower end of the wood, near one of the entrances from Redshoot. oak, with thorn undergrowth at the lower end – There is a fine sweet chestnut near Roe gate.

Sloden. a most romantic old wood of Yew, Whitebeam, oak, Beech, ash, Crab apple, holly, Thorn, Dogwood & Spindle; mistle-toe grows on the whitebeams on the N.W. side of Sloden Hill. All about here ancient banks & ditches tell of some sort of human activity. The track above Whiteshoot passes over a square site enclosed by a low bank & ditch. & Wise (p. 216) considers Sloden to have been the site of a Romano British settlement in connection with the potteries.

Note. The foliage of some of the small yew-trees in Sloden, is nibbled round so close as to give the effect of clipped bushes. I asked Broad of Amberwood if he had ever observed ill effects from such yew browsing. He said that according to his observation it was the top boughs of yew that were poisonous, & instanced 3 deer being found dead by him close beside some yew boughs that had been broken down by snow, & that had been eaten. The slots of deer in the snow, shewed that they had been eating the foliage of these broken boughs. (It was not the top boughs that were specially poisonous, but their normal effect upon an empty stomach)

Sloden Enclosure - planted in 1864. still enclosed. oak & Scots fir with occasional finely grown spruce, & larch.

Slufters. planted in 1862. still enclosed. Scots fir, with fine Spruce near the high road. Michael found a woodcock's nest, with eggs, beside one of the rides in 1906.

Studley. an old wood of beech & holly: at the North end, the Queen beech is said to be the finest grown beech tree in the Forest.

## Winding Stonehard. & Ocknell.

The Forest ponies that live among these hills & valleys & old enclosures, seem to be just as wild & indigenous as their surroundings. They are wild, in so far as they unbroken, & only to be caught by hunting them; but they are all owned; the agister would tell you by whom; & Further he would tell you where every pony should 'haunt'. That is his business. He it is who collects The modest payment of eighteen pence, which is the yearly fee for a pony from those owners who have Forest rights —

Only eighteen pence a-year! And this for the keep of a
mare who should make you a present annually of a foal!
Surely, you think, it must pay to keep Forest ponies.

So it would seem; yet when First we came here, I was
surprised to find that none of our small farmers had ponies
up in the Forest. They had tried it, they said, & it did
not pay. The ponies came down; strayed in the lanes;
were pounded; in short were more trouble than they were
worth — I wondered — Now, however I see that they are
right. If Forest ponies are to pay, you must either be

specially situated in the heart of the Forest; or, you must have
rough pastures, handy, where your ponies can be kept whe[n]
feed runs short in the winter; or, you must pick up the mu[?]
at very low prices.    For example.    Forest mares that
are good `haunters`, cost about £8 apiece. With luck
you get two foals in three years from each mare. These fet[ch]

Newland's Bridge

from £2 to £3.10, Sold at 5 months old as Suckers . Say a
mare has nine years of breeding life := during which time she
has six foals, of which you keep one filly foal to take her place
as a brood mare : that leaves five Suckers sold at an average
of — Say — £2.10 = £12.10 . From this deduct 13ˢ. 6 for
nine year's tailmarking . This leaves £11. 16. 6 - that is £3.16.6

profit on £8 spread over nine years. But this computation is too liberal. It supposes that you pay nothing for driving in your colts; for marking; that everything goes right with your mare & her six foals; & that she costs you nothing extra in feed during a hard winter. Again, if your mare comes down from the Forest, & strays, you soon spend both time & shillings in finding the wanderer — As, for instance, I spent a week in the spring of 1906, & ten shillings finding Jenny, whose thoughts had lightly turned to love, & been thus mis-led to Woodlands! Nine miles from here — And thus your margin of profit may vanish *

The larger pony owners generally turn out a stallion; & the mares are thus served free, & by chance; but the chance has been much improved of late years by the annual Forest pony shows at Lyndhurst, where prizes are given to the best

Here, we keep our mares partly out on the common & partly in: using them for six months of the year: and the better feed & care which they get commands a better price for the foals. (I have sold three suckers at £6 £5.10. & £6.10 respectively) But this breeding is limited by the feed on the common, & no one keeps more than two mares under these local conditions.

In the foregone note on Forest ponies the 'Agister' is mentioned, se Lewis p.32, et seq:, for definitions of the various duties of the Forest officers. Here, on the outskirts of Forest law, we have a loca

Officer of our own, also of Norman origin — The Hayward, the hedge (haie) guardian, who has the charge of stray beasts, who keeps the key of the pound, & takes the fine.

The 'poundage' fine in the case of strayed ponies is 4$^d$ and the pound keeper has no right to demand damages; that must be done by the person who has sustained the damage. (Verderor's C$^t$ November 19. 1906) at the same Court M$^r$ Evans said he had spent £1.9.6. last year reclaiming one mare & colt!

Besides the ponies, fallow deer are the principal wild oc-cupants of the Forest — Ponies — Deer — surely the last should be first? Surely the deer & the Forest are cause & effect — The Forest exists because of the deer, & the ponies are intruders. Well, there is reason in the inverted order that I have adopted. The deer have been dis-possessed. Since the deer removal Act of 1851 they are sup-posed to have been exterminated. The remnant of the ancient herds only exist on sufferance, & the ponies now legally roam in their stead. Truly a democratic vista, & a topsy-turvy event to grow out of the stern Forest laws of William the Conqueror.

In Gerald Lascelles' article on fallow deer in the Victoria History of Hampshire, he estimates their present (1900.) number in the Forest at about 200, more or less: but of late years they have increased considerably. There are four special haunts of the deer on our Northern side of the Forest. Roe, including Pinnick and Milkham. Sluflers. Holly Hatch & Anses. Island's Thorn

Woodford Bottom.

& Amberwood . If you know where to look for them, you
will rarely be disappointed . This year (1906) has been a
acorn year, & the deer congregated in the oak woods. Mor
deer were in Roe during this autumn & winter than had
been known for years : a herd of 57 was seen, & the keep
at Roe cottage put the number of fallow deer haunting in R
Milkham & Pinnick at more than 100 . Beatrix & I sau
a herd of 20 in Pinnick; Humphrey & I a herd of 18 in Hol
Hatch, so the deer still thrive in spite of their extermination

    When their number gets up — as it has now — they are
shot by the keepers (with grape-shot) as well as hunted by

he deer hounds, & when they trespass & damage crops the
forest Farmers shoot them also . I remember in 1899 staying
at Goulding's, at Highwood Farm, & after eating venison
for supper, I asked where it came from ? 'Shot on
my Farm . 'Lascellas' (so he pronounced Lascelles) 'he come
& says — Goulding I'm told you've a been shooting deer,
you mustn't do it' — 'Who's a going to stop me if they come
on my land ?' — 'Well, he says . you mustn't shoot the deer'
'Who's a going to stop me' ? I says — 'Well, he says, you
mustn't do it, & I shall tell Lord Narmanton' — So the
next time I pays my rent, I sent his Lordship a haunch

& told 'en I could-en keep the deer off my land, & he never said nothing —' And this confirmed Goulding in his interrogatory creed — who's a going to stop me ?

As to the red deer; 'the tall deer' which William the Conqueror 'loved as if he was their father', only a poor remnant remains to testify of the past . There were 7 hinds, 2 stags & a brocket known to be on this side of the Forest in 1906 –1907: and Spencer Holland & I saw the stags & the brocket in Anses in the autumn of 1906 . I have never seen roe-deer in the Forest, but there are said to b some occasionally — strayed from Dorset where they are fairly plentiful, especially on the wooded slopes a combes of Bulbarrow, where I have twice seen them .

The two harvests of the Forest are Fern & holly — ferning in the autumn, hollying in the winter .

The fern is cut by the Forest men, & carried by the buyers at 8/ a load [s * p.117] : & the loads are full measure ! Twelve feet high from the ground, bonded in the load corded, & then the moving brown stacks creak slowl homeward along the rutty Forest tracks to supply litte for the small farmers who are not men of straw .

Forest litter; is the coarse grass cut in the enclosu rides, & this also we buy of the Forest men at 9s a load [* s.n. p.1]

Hollying begins at the end of November. The holly-trees are chosen in each walk & cut by the woodm chosen & cut I should have written, as the hollyer has to say in the matter — Then the man who has undertaken to buy the holly, cuts up the felled trees into 'Forest faggots' (12 bundles go to a faggot.) for which he pays £10 per 100 faggots to the Crown. John Thomas of Furzehill takes Burley walk, & he & his 5 helpers aim at cutting up, tieing, & carting home to Gorley 30 faggots a day — and this for the fortnight during which the work lasts. The holly is then all taken to the nearest station, & trained up to Nine Elms yard, where it is sold to the various buyers. A Forest faggot is said to cost the seller about 5/ by the time it is on sale in London, and the trade sale price varies from 5/6 to 6/6 . This year (1907.) some of the holly was poor stuff with few berries and hollyers lost money — £60 is said to have been lost by a man at Bartley — The crown deals well with its holly tenants, & an old hollyer continues year by year to get the walk which he has been wont to take. John Thomas tells of a man from up-along who wanted terrible to get into the business, so he wrote & bid £12 a hundred faggots — instead of the £10 which we do give — but they told 'en that they must first satisfy their old customers, & then he mid have the holly that wasn't wanted at the price he named — So he got our leavings drav —

Both these prices on p.116. include cartage — i.e. delivered here.

As to the timber, & the actual management of the woods from the afforesting point of view, I am not competent to write.

117.

Hiscock's Hill.

The subject needs special knowledge which I do not posse Lascelles — the deputy Surveyor — gives an account of his charge in the 2nd volume of The Victoria History of Hampshire and his record is not very encouraging ——

Well, I have now given some account of our side of the Forest though neither words nor pictures can convey the charm, the var -iety, the monotony, the tenacity of the life that abides in these wild places — The heath passes from dun to sombre green, then blooms in purple & withers to rusty grey — The brake push up their crosiers in May, make green patchwork on the dark hills through the summer, yellow through the autumn bleached-brown through the winter — The bog myrtle flowers

i dull red & rust, then becomes 'sweet gale' in leafy fragrance,
hen gilds the brown streams with borders of gold — The
og-moss passes from green to yellow to orange to red —
he furze passes from flowery radiance, to prickly dulness —
the mat-grass from glaucous to sandy green — and the woods
. The woods pass from the infinite variety of winter branch
bud colour, to the brightness of spring, to the fulness of
ummer, to the splendour of autumn — So the years
ass, & I, who also pass, say grace for this infinite
reation, dimly perceived, yet beloved; & dream of
he secret inlet which will unite us to the sights, &
ounds, & scents of Mother Earth —

120.

*Looking South from Sloden Hill.*

"Jock, when ye hae naething        else to do, ye may be aye sticking
in a tree – it will be                    growing. Jock, when ye're
sleeping" – last words             of the Laird of Dumbiedikes

122.

# Pomona

The old Saxon Coronation Benediction is thus given in "The book of the Apple"; "Bless, O Lord, the courage of this Prince, & prosper the work of his hands; & by thy blessing may this land be filled with Apples, with the Fruit & dew of heaven, from the top of the ancient mountains, from the Apples of the eternal hills, from the fruits of the earth & its fulness"— So when our land is filled with apples in the autumn, & the laden branches are trigged-up to bear their burden, & the orchard grass is spotted with fallen fruit, the blessing invoked a thousand years ago is still received in the ruddy gift of Pomona.

Yet — I must confess — This tribute comes from an

unworthy worshipper"! Alas, I cannot eat an apple. Dire pains ensue — No, my pleasure is vicarious, & I grow apples for others to eat, & praise the goddess at a distance. Still my love of apples is not wholly platonic for though Eve may not now tempt me, Noah does, and good cider is to my taste the very best of all our native drinks. The amber juice is pressed from the heart of a hundred sunny days; it recalls sights & scents of the orchard's wealth; and the keen, mellow draught comes from the bountiful breasts of the very goddess herself, — Pomona —      But remember — there is cider & cider I do not write the praises of the usual commercial beverage — bottled cider — sparkling cider — 'our native champagne' & such like — My best cider is pure apple juice, fermented, without any addition, & kept in a cask on draught.

In cider-making the first consideration must be given to the apples. You must not expect to get a good result from a heap of rotting windfalls. Codlings, Pearmains, Sweet Russets, Orange Pippins, Prophets, & Davys, are the apples that we mostly use for cider — The best combination I have yet to learn. Where the apples come from must also be taken into consideration. — They should come from good strong land, for the fruit of apple-trees growing on a gravelly soil makes a white

& watery cider. Rockborne apples, from the Radcliffe's orchard, make excellent cider. Our apples, & Furze hill apples, good cider. Ibsley apples, bad cider. — Besides the apples, consider the cask. An old spirit, port, or sherry cask is best. Avoid any other: & cider in an old cider cask is not so good as cider in a new spirit, port, or sherry cask. — by 'new', I mean new to cider as its content. The best cider that I ever made here, was in a rum cask, made from Rockborne apples.

Now for the making — Apples, ruddy, green & golden lie around in heaps: slabs of pomace, speck- ed, brown & yellow, tell of the cider-press: the same tale is told by the faint, pervading smell of sweet malic juice which is being squeezed from the crushed fruit: & the cider-makers grind the apples, & work the press, & ladle the brown liquid from the receiving tubs into the casks, till their long sacking aprons are splashed with signs of every stage of the making — pips, & rind, & pomace, & apple juice— and so they win the gift of Pomona.

The apple-grinder; The cider-press; The tubs; The peck; & the casks, are the necessary plant for this job of cider-making — They must all be as clean as hard scrubbing can make them. Then, first, the trough

The Apple-mill.

of the apple-grinder is filled with a sack of apples, then two
men work the handles of the wheel, & the heap of apples
in the trough quickly sink through the slicing cogs of the
hand-mill, & fall as pulp into the receiving tub. Then
this pulp is shovelled into a rough, horsehair cloth, neat-
ly folded, and the package is put into the press. Seven
times is this shovelling & folding repeated with seven
cloths, & with the seventh of such packings of pulp,
the press is filled. The top is then put on, & the
press screws are then lowered by two men, who work
them by means of wooden winches on either side of
of the press. As the pressure increases, the applejuice
begins to flow from a vent-hole at the bottom of the

The press.

 press, & it is caught by a receiving tub. Then, when the
last turn of the screws has been exacted, the press is left
to drain off the final drippings of the expressed juice.
Now another sack of apples is reduced to pulp by the
grinder — Then the men return to the squeezed-out
press — It is unscrewed, & the first lot of pulp is taken
out, & put back in the now empty trough of the apple
grinder — Again the men return to the press; the pulp
of the second sack is wrapped according to the same
method in the horsehair cloths, & pressed in the same
manner as the first — Then, on completion, the second
lot of pulp is taken out of the press, put in the trough
with the first lot, & both are ground together for the

127.

second time, & afterwards both lots, (now ground & pressed into half their first compass,) are put into the press together & pressed for the second time — Thus every drop of juice is squeezed & crushed from the pulp which has by this time been compressed into slabs of brown pomace — only fit for pig food — The liquor that runs from the press into the receiving tub, is of a muddy golden colour; the darker it is, the better hopes have the cider makers of the supposed quality of the cider; when it is full — by 'it' I mean the receiving tub — it is carried to the cask, & its contents are baled out in the peck, then poured on the head of the cask, whence the liquor runs into the cask through the bung-hole.   Two sacks of apples

128.

The top of the Press — They say that this will stand a
pressure of 30 tons — The press cost £20, 37 years ago.

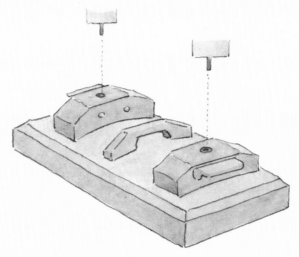

...ake about 22 to 24 gallons of cider — The horse-
...air cloths are needed to strain off the pips & pulp
...hich otherwise would find their way into the liquor; these
...loths cost 7ˢ 6ᵈ each, & only last about 2 years:
...hey shrink considerably under their usage — When
...he cask is filled, it is carted away to its destination,
...nd is then put away in a cool place to ferment — This
...ermentation goes on for about a fortnight or three weeks,
...nd, during that time, the top of the cask head is covered
...ith the cider froth that rises up through the open
...ung hole with a soft hissing sound; gradually this
...eases, & the froth subsides, then the bung may be
...riven in. & the cider may now be left to clear. In

6 weeks it will be drinkable, but will not be clear & bright for 3 or 4 months — Such is the way that cider is made here — apple juice, pure & simple — and the result being so good, of course cunning housewives think to improve on it by dodges — such as adding pricked raisins, sugar, or cloves before the cider has finished fermen-ing: and then they dignify the drink with the name of cider - wine — but I do not like it, as I said before, my best cider is pure apple juice, fermented, without any addition, & kept in a cask on draught — see note p.1

    'In good apple year's 'Captain' Thomas goes about, round, & up - along for 6 weeks in the autumn making cider for the small farmers & the cottagers. 6ᵈ a gallon is the price he usually charges me for both supplying the apples, making the cider, & delivering the casks here. This year, 1907, his charge is 8ᵈ a gallon as apples are so scarce, & he made for me 3 half hogs-head 'caskés', containing 30 to 32 gallons apiece. Notwithstanding its excellence — as I think — cider is not held in high estimation about here. Actually, brewer's beer to wit, Strong's of Romsey — is supposed to be a more hospitable drink to supply at a supper ! Hot cider is preferred to cold : and is considered to be a sovereign remedy for chills — especially if drunk when you are abed. Still, I suppose the demand for cider mus e increasing. For within the last year or two Strong's have supplied a commercial cider, (which may possess the virtue of keeping, but which does not taste like pure apple-juice,) and so "the fruit & dew of heaven" may even now be obtained at a tied house !

On the day that I made these sketches of cider-making at Furze Hill, I looked in to see 'Mother' – Mrs Thomas, by her fireside. She was terrible rough, but, as usual, soon brisked up in conversation. The uncertainty of riches was our topic – "My father", she said, "he oughter had property in Brighton: his mother was a widder, & she never would tell en about the writins of this here property. but kep on how she'd tell en as soon as she was a dyin – Well, she was took with a see-sure, & never know'd nothing, nor never come to, bonified, as you mid say, tho' they threw all the fire-irons down-stairs to try & give her a start, if so be she mid come to, but she never took no notice, & died without being able to tell en – Well, there was a poor sorter butcher feller at Horsham, he dealed in half dead cows & things, he was trustee, & he set up grand all on a sudden, & his son was quite the gentleman & took to huntin' – So he must a know'd where the writin's was, & must a used 'im as he know'd how."

Home made cider suggests other home made drinks, –such as 'home-brew' & home made wine, so, having just

131.

made one digression, I shall continue with another. Everywhere & always habitual beverage is a matter of no small importance, & I believe that Temperantia & the Universal Digestion would benefit if home-brew & light cider ousted brewer's beer & Tea — Brewer's beer is — well, just brewer's beer, neither refreshing, palatable, nor digestible, but intoxicating — Tea is tannin & Indigestion; drunk freely at every meal; & poured from a tea-pot that has stood stewing on the hob for half an hour — keeping warm for 'Father' — Perhaps you demur — Cider & home-brew are intoxicants — Well Southey, I think, said of Wordsworth that his standard of intoxication was miserably low, yet I doubt whether he would ever have achieved his low standard on our cider or home-brew, For they are not potent beverages, & are much more wholesome than any other habitual drinks that a poor man can obtain — Of course his tea need not be stewed — only it is, has been, & will be — for such mis-guided decoction is in the cottage nature of things.

William Cobbett is perhaps a doubtful ally — doubt-ful, because he was such an unreasonable fellow & such a brilliant writer — & he hated too much. Cursed are 'machine brewers', Tea, Potatoes, Bankers, Paper money, 'The Wen', (London) 'The System', etc, etc, etc, till his reader refuses any responsive 'Amen', & Cobbett is condemned as a common Scold. Still, he knew ~

132.

something about cottage economy — even tho' his own was at fault — & he was as temperate in living, as he was intemperate in speech, so I raise his turbulent ghost in witness — Cobbetts Cottage Economy. published in 1828. Contains much useful information as to home brewing, brilliant praise of home-made beer, racy abuse of 'machine brewers', & fierce attacks on tea-drinkers — I must add the sub-title of Cottage Economy, which is very characteristic of Cobbett, the hard rider of hobbies — ' Containing Information relative to the brewing of Beer, making of Bread, keeping of Cows, Pigs, Bees, Ewes, Goats, Poultry & Rabbits, & relative to other matters deemed useful in the conducting of the affairs of a Labourer's Family = to which are added, Instructions relative to the selecting, the cutting, & the bleaching of the Plants of English Grass & Grain, for the purpose of making Hats & Bonnets = and also Instructions for erecting & using Ice-houses, after the Virginian manner. ' ! I will not quote Cobbett's information as to home brewing, as it is accessible, but I will tell how James Hayter of South Gorley makes his home brewed. First, 25 gallons of water are heated to boiling point in a copper — Then the boiling water is ladled out into a tub, at the bottom out side of which there is a draw off tap, the passage of the tap being protected on the in side

133.

by a sort of wicker cage, called 'a muck'. When the steam of the boiling water has sufficiently subsided for Stayter to see his face in it, he considers that the right temperature has arrived for the malt to be added — an important point as the malt must not be scalded — A full bushel of malt is then added to the 25 gallons of water, thoroughly stirred, & then the contents of the tub are left to soak all night.          In the morning, the liquor, now called 'sweet wort', is drawn off by the tap — 'the muck' preventing the outflow of malt grains — & put in the copper. One lb: of hops is added, & the sweet wort & hops are boiled for an hour in the copper — The liquor is then dipped out, & poured into a tub, through a 'range', i.e., a sort of strainer.          It is left to cool to about milk heat, & then a pint of balm is added. The balm should work for about 2 or 3 days — There should be a good unbroken head of working balm on the top of the tub, & before it sinks, the beer should be drawn off, & put in the barrel — It should not be corked down tight, as the beer may ferment a little after having been put in the barrel. The malt grains are good food for pigs —

          Now for my other digression from 'Pomona' namely, home made wine — which we make every year from the grapes that grow on the vines planted in 1893 against the house (Muscadines.) & against the studio (Foster's seedling

134.

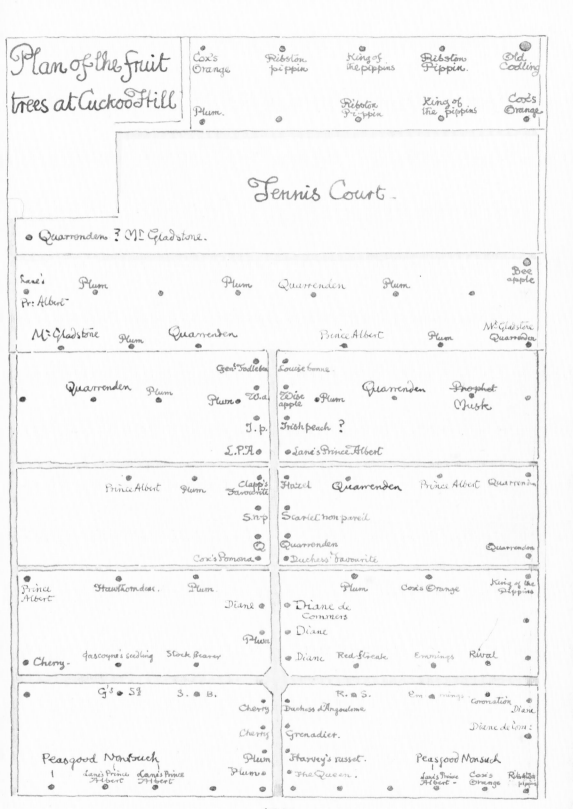

**Plan of the fruit trees at Cuckoo Hill**

| Cox's Orange | Ribston pippin | King of the pippins | Ribston Pippin | Old Codling |
| Plum. | | Ribston Pippin | King of the pippins | Cox's Orange |

**Tennis Court.**

Quarrenden ? Mr Gladstone.

| Lane's Pr: Albert | Plum | Plum | Quarrenden | Plum | Bee apple |
| Mr Gladstone | Plum | Quarrenden | | Prince Albert | Plum | Mr Gladstone Quarrenden |

| Quarrenden | Plum | Plum | W.a | Genl Todleben | Louise bonne | | | |
| | | | J. p. | Wise apple | Plum | Quarrenden | Prophet Musk |
| | | | L.P.A | Irish peach ? | | | |
| | | | | Lane's Prince Albert | | | |

| Prince Albert | Plum | Clapp's Favourite | Hazel | Quarrenden | Prince Albert | Quarrenden |
| | | S.n.p | Scarlet non pareil | | | |
| | | Q | Quarrenden | | | Quarrenden |
| | Cox's Pomona | Duchess' Favourite | | | |

| Prince Albert | Hawthorn dean. | Plum | | Plum | Cox's Orange | King of the Pippins |
| | | Diane | Diane de Conners | | |
| | | | Diane | | |
| | | Plum | | | |
| Cherry. | Gascoyne's seedling | Stock Bearer | Diane | Red streak | Emmings | Rival |

| G's S2 | S. B. | | R. S. | Em mings | Coronation Diane |
| | Cherry | Duchess d'Angoulome | | Diane de com: |
| | Cherry | Grenadier. | | |
| Peasgood Nonsuch | Plum | Harvey's russet. | Peasgood Nonsuch | |
| 1 Lane's Prince Albert | Lane's Prince Albert | Plum | The Queen. | Lane's Prince Albert - | Cox's Orange | Ribston pippin |

Here is our recipe — Allow 6 lbs of grapes to 1 gallon of water — Crush the grapes, & put them into a pan — Pour boiling water over them — Let them soak for 24 hours — Strain, & press the grapes to extract what juice may remain — Allow 3 lbs of lump sugar to a gallon of the liquor — Mix well & put into a jar, or small barrel — Leave the liquor to ferment for about a fortnight — When the fermentation has ceased, cork the jar or small barrel, & let the wine stand thus for some months before bottling. Our wine is of pink amber colour, & has a fresh grape flavour that gives it quite a desert character _____ But I must not close my chapter on Pomona with such digressions — I must return to apples, and shall end — as I began — with a quotation. Gerard, writing in 1597, says "I have seene in the pastures & hedgerowss about the grounds of a worshipfull Gentleman dwelling two miles from Hereford called M. Roger Bodnome, so many trees of all sortes, that the servantes drinke for the most part no other drinke, but that which is made of Apples. The quantitie is such, that by the report of the Gentleman himselfe, the Parson hath for Tithe many hogsheads of Syder. .... An example doubt-lesse to be followed of Gentlemen that have land & living: (but envie saith, the poore will breake downe our hedges, & we shall have the least part of the fruit ) but forward in the name of God, graffe, set, plant & nourish up trees in every corner of your grounds, the labour is small, the cost is nothing, the commoditie is great, your selves shall have plentie, the poore shall have somewhat in time of want to relieve their necessitie, and God shall reward your good mindes & diligence.'

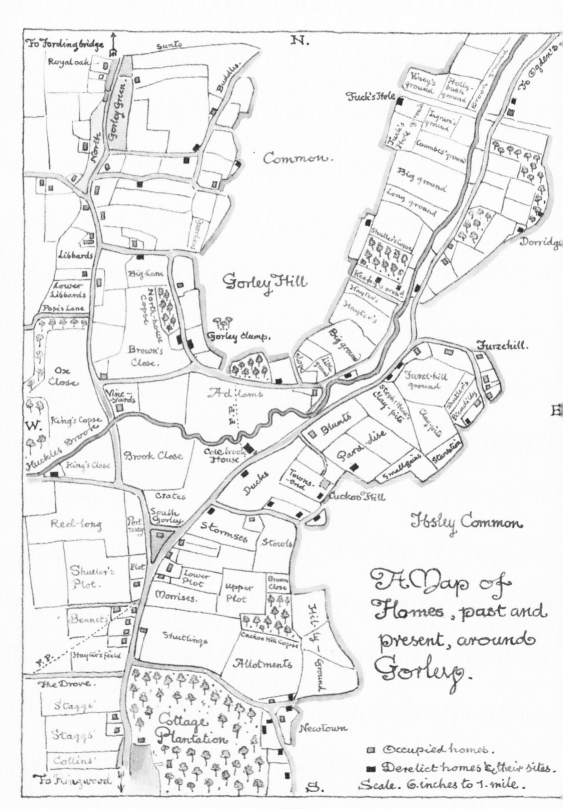

N.

To Fordingbridge
Royal oak
sunto
Buddles
To Ogden's
Wisey's ground
Holly-bush ground
Brook-ground
Fuck's Hole
Ingram's ground
North
Gorley Green
Common.
Fuck's Hole to Fordingbridge
Coombes' ground
Big ground
Long ground
Dorridge
Geckoes'
Gorley Hill
Shutler's Copse
Libbards
Big Lane
Keep's orch'd
Lower Libbards
North-house Copse
Hayter's
Hayter's
Pope's Lane
Gorley Clump.
Big ground
Furzehill.
Brown's Close.
Furze-hill ground
Shutler's Piccadilly
Ox Close
Vine-yards
Adlams
slong
little ground
Stephen's clay-pits
Clay-pits
W.
King's Copse Brook
Blunts
Paradise
E.
Huckles Brook
King's Close
Brook Close
Cole-brook House
Ducks
Smallgains
Stanestan
Crates
Towns-end
Cuckoo Hill
Red-long
Port way
South Gorley
Stormses
Stowls
Ibsley Common
Shutler's Plot.
Plot
Lower Plot
Upper Plot
Broom Close
A Map of
Bennet's
Morrises.
Hill-y Ground
Homes, past and
present, around
F.P.
Hayter's field
Stutlings
Cuckoo Hill Copse
Allotments
Gorley.
The Drove.
Stagg's
Stagg's
Cottage Plantation
Newtown
Collins'
Occupied homes.
To Ringwood
Derelict homes & their sites.
S.
Scale. 6 inches to 1 mile.

138.

# Mutability

But Times do change & move continually :
So nothing heere long standeth in one stay :
Wherefore this lower world who can deny
But to be subject still to Mutability ?  Spenser.


There can be no doubt that, 100 years ago, these hill-
-sides were more thickly populated than they are now.
Look at the map on the opposite page . It only covers
a space of country 1½ mile long, by 1 mile wide, & yet
within that small area 35 homes have vanished during
the last hundred years , while only 13 new homes have
arisen in the same area to replace the 35.
Why is this ? What can be the reason for so great a change
befalling a locality within the knowledge of living men ?
Well, like most changes & chances of this mortal life
in which many causes contribute to the happening of this
or that , so here , custom, conduct, & character all help
to account for the fact of these derelict homes .
The origin of most of these homes happened in this way –
Land was grabbed on the edge of the common by a

139.

squatter. Here, on a bit of heather waste, he hastily reared a mud-walled cottage. Then he reclaimed the land made a garden, & then the Lord of the Manor stepped in, — before the squatter had occupied for 20 years — & claimed rent in token of his over-Lordship.

The usual custom was to grant such squatters a lease of his holding for 3 lives at a nominal rental — in consideration of work done in grubbing, building, and reclaiming — But mud-walled cottages built in haste, will not stand for a long future; and by the time that the 3 lives had fallen, the mud-walls were likewise tottering to their fall; so it came to pass that when these lifeholds fell into the possession of the Lord of the Manor, he was confronted with a 'damnosa hæreditas'. The lives had fallen, the cottage was falling, what was to be done? _____ The chance of the Times decided. The fact that such homes bred up boys & girls who were compelled by their circumstances to deal with country life in a capable manner was ignored. The fact that such homes were tumble-down, & their inmates were rather independant was remembered. The ideal of breeding capable country-men & women was not to the fore when the leases fell in. New tenants, (or the old ones,) would want new buildings — They would be

possible paupers & probable poachers ___ And so, with
all England, awakening to the glories of machines & larger ven-
-tures, no wonder that a Lord of the Manor should
think that 'Ichabod' was writ large on the old customs
of tenure; should follow the bent of his generation, &
throw his troublesome small-holdings into larger holdings
___ which were readily taken up by able tenant farmers
with a balance at their bankers, & without demands
for innumerable scattered buildings.

From the point of view of the Lord of the Manor, the
old squatter population was not blameless. They aided
& abetted the smugglers*. They knew something of deer
stealing, & of free-living on the edge of the Forest.
Anyhow, I seem to see that there was no live op-
-inion to back the Lord of the Manor in taking a far-seeing

Note.
* Jas Hayter can mind finding his father's horses one early morning all in a
muck & sweat, & when he asked his father why? he was told to ask no questions
___ but a keg of brandy, left in the manger, gave him an answer ___ It
was thus that the smugglers said 'thankyou', when they were hard pressed
by the excisemen, & commandeered fresh horses for their 'run'.

method of conducting his affairs — when all the tumble-down life-hold property came into hand — He took the line of least resistance; the squatter's cottages were left in occupation till they tumbled down, & then the little holding were added to larger holdings. Such, in brief, is the chronicle of the vanished hearths that once skirted the commons.

Further Note on Smuggling. In Sept. 1747 'The three Brothers' cutter, laden with a cargo of brandy, rum & tea, run by John Diamond was captured by the privateer 'Swift', Capt. Johnson, & the smuggled goods lodged in the custom house at Poole. John Diamond was leader of a gang of smugglers from Charlton Forest, in the S.E. of Hampshire, & early in Oct. the whole gang — 60 men — met at Rowland's Castle, rode to Lyndhurst, where they rested for a day, then, while 30 of their number guarded the roads, the remaining 30 rode on the night of Oct. 7. to Poole, broke open the Customs House & recovered the tea, but left the spirits. Next day the smugglers returned with their booty through Fordingbridge where a crowd was assembled to see the cavalcade, among the crowd was Daniel Chater, a shoe-maker known to Diamond, having worked with him harvesting, so they shook hands, & Diamond gave him some tea. The smugglers baited, & then went on by Sandy Balls to Brook, where they divided up the run tea by weight, each man getting 5 bags apiece — equal to £12.10 — a bag being worth 50ˢ —

Shortly after this daring exploit, His Majesty's Proclamation came out offering a reward for the apprehension of the persons who broke open the custom's house at Poole, & Diamond being suspected was taken into custody at Chichester. Then the customs authorities at Southampton were told that Diamond had been recognised by Chater in Fordingbridge, the upshot being that Wm Galley (a custom's officer) was sent with Danl Chater to Major Battin a Sussex magistrate, bearing with them a letter from the Collector of Customs to the Major requesting him to examine Chater with reference to what he knew of the affair. Major Battin was staying at Stanstead near Roland's Castle, & on the way there, Galley & Chater stopped at the White Hart in Roland's Castle, drank, gossipped, & let out that they were the bearers of a letter to Major Battin. This aroused the suspicion of the landlady of the inn, (who was the mother of two reputed smugglers) so she sent out to call some of the gang, while she detained Galley & Chater pretending that her son who had gone out had taken the stable key. Seven smugglers assembled at The White Hart in answer to the landlady's warning. Galley & Chater were plied with drink, & eventually they fell into a drunken sleep — the letter was taken from them — read — & so their mission was known for certain by the smugglers. To omit all details, but under circumstances of prolonged brutality both Galley & Chater were killed by the smugglers. Galley was buried at Rake near Rogate, secretly, by night. Chater was flung down Harris' well in Ladyholt Park, near Charlton. The prolonged absence from home of these two men aroused suspicion, a proclamation was issued offering a reward, and eventually information was forthcoming that resulted in the capture, trial, & execution of all the murderers — This story is taken from "A full & genuine History of the inhuman & unparallel'd Murders committed on the Bodies of Mr William Galley a customhouse officer in the Port of Southampton and Mr Daniel Chater a shoemaker of Fordingbridge in Hampshire. 1749" a grim little book, that gives a vivid picture of smuggling & of its demoralising effect. It was no game. Not hide & seek on a manly scale; but a school for desperate criminals on the one hand, & for despicable informers on the other — From the same book I take the following statement of "Little Harry" — "The Master Smugglers contract for the goods with the Master of a cutter that fetches them & the Master of the cutter fixes a Time & Place where he designs to land. As the Master Smugglers cannot fetch all the Goods themselves, so they hire Men whom they call their Riders; & they allow each Man half a Guinea a Journey, & bear all Expenses of eating & drinking & Horse, & an Allowance of a Dollop of Tea (40 lb weight. worth 25s.) & they always make one Journey, sometimes two, &

sometimes three in a Week; which is indeed such a Temptation that very few People in the Country could withstand ____ all the Smugglers both Masters & Riders drink Drams to great Excess, & generally kept themselves half drunk; which was the only Thing that occasioned them to commit such Outrages as they did sometimes ____

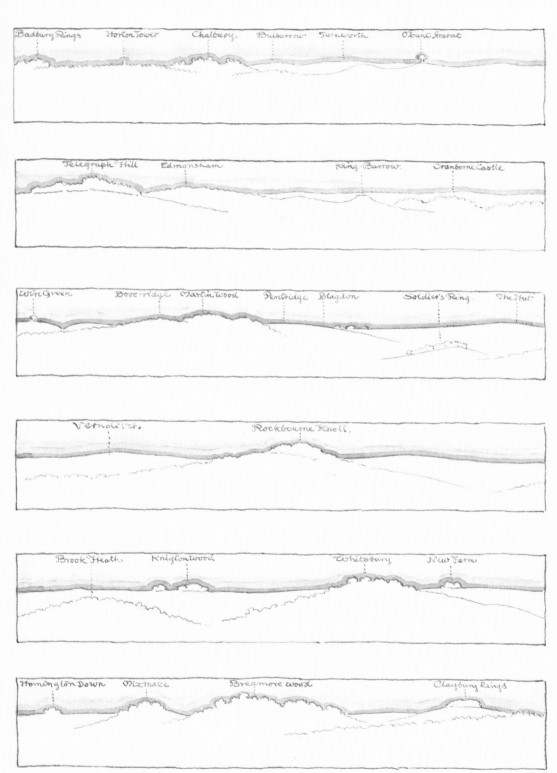

Outline of the Chase horizon, as seen from Robin Hood's Clump — Left to right

146.

# Cranborne Chase

Our days here begin over the Forest, & end behind the Chase. Eastward, at the back of Cuckoo Hill, lies the New Forest. Westward, in front, rises the horizon of Cranborne Chase. We look across the Avon Valley = over 3 counties — Hampshire, Dorsetshire, & Wiltshire — towards hills, dim, with the enchantment of distance = fold upon fold of chalk upland, stretching from Clayburg & Verndifch in the North, to Rushmore & Shaftesbury in the West, with Badbury Rings just rising above Holt Forest to mark the Southern outbounds of the Chase.
— Forest & Chase — What is the difference? The distinction, according to Manwood, is that a Forest was constituted & possessed by the King only, & was not subject to the common law, having Forest courts & special laws of its own, whereas a Chase might be held by a subject, & had only customs & privileges — not laws of its own — It was controlled by the common law. Now, Cranborne Chase is only a place name, a memory; it has been disfranchised. The Forest survives,

147.

but the Chase has ceased to exist, & most of the district is cultivated as sheep & corn farms : yet still it retains a character of spacious wildness — & the different sort of wildness of the Chase & of the Forest is very remarkable : the one is an upland tract of chalk, with clay caps on the hills which rise to 800 feet on the ox-drove ridge way ; a cold land, wind swept; a land of rolling downs where sheep-bells tinkle & larks sing ; a land of barrows, & pit dwellings, & dykes, of scattered yews, & thorns, & juniper ; of woodlands — oak & ash, with hazel undergrowth, such as you will not see from end to end of the Forest; of chalk streams that barely flow during five months of the year — The other is a wood & heathland whose highest hills are only 400 feet above the sea, channeled by many little streams, now rushing, now trickling over gravelly beds — a land of gravel, sand, & clay with a mild climate, and though these two tracts of country adjoin — on either side of the Avon — it would be difficult to find a more complete change of scene than is presented by Cranborne Chase and the New Forest —

The earliest record of Cranborne Chase is in the year 1216 when its perambulation was commanded by King John. These ancient limits are further recorded in a map by Richard Harding of Blandford 1618, (reproduced in The Chronicles of Cranborne,) wherein Cranborne Chase is shewn bounded by the Avon, the Allen, the Stour, the Fontmel brook, &

the Nadder = a circuit of nearly 100 miles = containing 72 parishes & 10.000 people = more than 20 miles across, & stretching from Blandford to Salisbury, where cheminage toll used to be taken on Harnham Bridge by the lord of the Chase _ These were the 'outer bounds' _ The 'inner bounds', shewn on this same map, include a district stretching from Woodyates to West Lodge = about 27 miles in circuit = 10 miles long & 4 miles wide _

The Owners of the Chase have been the following ____
The Earls of Gloucester, from earliest records to ___
1461. Edward IV. & the Crown till James I granted it ___
1618. to the Earl of Salisbury whose descendant sold it ___
1671 to the Earl of Shaftesbury who sold it _____
1698 to Thos Freke of Shroton from whom it came by lineal descent
1714 to Lord Rivers _
(To the Chase belonged a Court for the preservation of Vert & Venison _ This was held by the Earl of Salisbury at Cranborne, by the Earl of Shaftesbury at Wimborne St Giles', & by Thos Freke & Lord Rivers at Rushmore _)
There are long records of many law-suits relating to the Chase, its bounds, & its privileges _ Deer-stealing frays were constantly occurring _ At length the friction of these proceedings, & the lawless-ness of this great district resulted in an Act of Parliament (9 George IV) by which the Chase was disfranchised. From Michaelmas 1829

Lord Rivers & his heirs were to receive £1800 clear annual rent, (charged on the Chase land,) in return for which all his privileges should be for ever extinguished. — Thus, as I have said, Cranborne Chase is now only a memory.

Broadly, we may regard the heathlands of Hampshire & Dorsetshire as virgin soil. — They shew no signs of having been cultivated or inhabited — excepting the district occupied by the New Forest potteries, & a few scattered barrows. — But the great chalk uplands of Cranborne Chase tell a very different tale. — They tell of settled life on these hills at a period when the valleys were swamps. — They tell of a great death roll, commemorated by mounds that still remain as land marks. — They tell of tribes of men, united & capable, who dug huge barrier dykes & mounds, winding across the downs. — And they tell of a more peaceful age, when the Roman road was made from Durnovaria to Sorbiodunum cutting through these mounds & dykes of an earlier race. — Cranborne Chase was in the way, & was held to be a desirable land through all the vague centuries of early men, while the Forest was ever neglected & out of the way, waste land, in sæculo sæculorum, by reason of its useless soil. —

Now here — as in my chapter on the Forest — I do not purpose to collect information that can be obtained elsewhere. — For example, to copy extracts from Chafin's Anecdotes of Cranborne

150.

Chase — Hoare's Wiltshire Antiquities — Hutchins' History of Dorset — A Chronicle of Cranborne — Warne's Index & Illustrated map of Dorsetshire its vestiges, Celtic, Roman, Saxon & Danish — or from General Pitt Rivers researches — These are books that should be consulted first-hand: but my purpose in the following pages is to give some suggestion of the present aspect of this wonderful stretch of ancient England, dinted with pit-dwellings, seamed with primæval earthworks, & haunted by memorable place-names — Vindogladia — Mons Badonicus alias Badbury Rings — Bokerly Dyke — Grims-ditch — Claybury Rings — Soldier's Rings — Whitsbury Camp — Breamore Miz Maze — Cranborne Castle — Ackling Dyke or Ikenield Street — Such names recal visions of the deserted handiwork of our forefathers, set among the spacious downs of Cranborne Chase: and as Time & the persistent plough will surely leave less than I see to another generation, it may be that the following pages of pictures — topographical pictures — will record more than I can now rightly guess. At the outset I will briefly sketch the sequence of these early men whose marks still remain on Cranborne Chase. Such outline may serve the purpose of a glossary of terms — to forestall explanations —

151.

<u>The old stone men</u> inhabited Britain when it was joined to the continent & when it stood 600 feet higher than it stands now. They were hunters with weapons of roughly chipped stone. Their records are found in the drift gravel of the Pleistocene period, & in caves. Their era is computed at 50.000 years. The Eskimos are supposed to be their descendants.

<u>The new stone men</u> inhabited Britain when it was an island. They intro-duced domestic animals, & were herdsmen as well as hunters. They used finely polished stone weapons. They lived in pit dwellings & made great cattle camps on the downs. They were small & dark with long skulls, & buried their dead in long barrows. Their era lasted from about B.C. 3000 to B.C 1000. The Finns, The Basques, & the people of S.W. Wales & S.W. Ireland are their descendants.

They were succeeded by a race of men with round skulls who used <u>Bronze</u> weapons, who buried their dead in round barrows, & who had a form of religion — Stonehenge & Avebury are their witness.

Claybury Ring & Grim's ditch.
from New Court Down.

During the bronze period continental races of Goidels & Brythons invaded Britain, & introduced Iron weapons. The Roman occupation lasted from A.D. 43. to A.D. 410. The Romans introduced the rectilinear plan in their camps & dwellings, & point to point planning in their roads. On their departure a distracted period ensued, The Jutes, The Angles, & the Saxons successively invaded & occupied parts of Britain – A.D. 830. The Danes began their raids on Britain, & the contest between the Anglo Saxon & the Dane continued till Wm the Conqueror settled the issue in 1066.

Claybury, or Clearbury Ring is on a chalk hill, 460 ft high, at the N.E extremity of Cranborne Chase. Its bank & ditch (40 feet high from top to bottom) encloses a sunken area of 5 acres, covered with beech & scots firs. There is a steep lynchet on the down, 50 yards from the camp ditch on the S.W side, elsewhere obliterated by cultivation. Sir R.C. Hoare attributes this camp to the West Saxons, & dates it about 519. A.D.

The Miz Maze        Breamore down

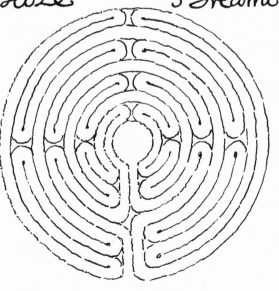

In Hereford Cathedral there is a 13th Century map of the world on which, amongst many strange geographical shapes, is figured the island of Crete, with a Labyrinth plan, & the inscription 'Labor- intus id est domus Dealli'. The Breamore Miz Maze is simi- lar to this Hereford Labyrinth plan, & also to the following grass-cut mazes in England, at Alkborough. Lincolnshire. at Bough- ton Green. Northants _ at Ripon Common (now destroyed) & to the following pavement mazes in French churches, St Quentin, Char- tres, & to one that is incised at Lucca.

Such widespread Tradition excites curiosity, so I shall try to ans- wer the question "Where did our Miz Maze come from?"

The device of a Labyrinth first appears in the 5th or 6th century B.C. on Cretan coins: and the earliest that we read of was 'the Cretan Labyrinth built by Dædalus in imitation of a more ancient labyrinth in Egypt by command of King Minos _ First it served as a prison for the monster Minotaur; then, as an architectural web to enclose Dædalus, whence he was enabled to escape by the aid of artificial wings'(Trollope Journal of Archaeology. vol XV) _ Herodotus describes an Egyptian architectural Labyrinth at Lake Mœris _ Pliny alludes to an architectural Labyrinth for royal sepulchres both in the island of Lemnos & of Samos _ Thus the early uses of Labyrinths seem to have been as prisons, & as burial places.

The Labyrinth at Lucca, already referred to, marks a new departure in the signification of the design. It is incised on the

porch pier of the Cathedral. The centre is filled by Theseus & the Minotaur (nearly effaced), & at the side is the following inscription
"Hic quem Creticus edit Dedalus est Laberintus,
De quo nullus vadere quivit qui fuit intus,
Ni Theseus gratis Ariane stamine jutus_
The Church now further appropriated the Pagan Labyrinth; & instead of the Minotaur, 'Sancta Ecclesia', or the Cross was inscribed as the centre of the design, which was deemed to be indicative of the complicated folds of sin by which man is sur--rounded, & how impossible it would be to extricate himself from them except through the assisting hand of Providence. Labyrinths were then frequently laid down in coloured marbles on church floors, e.g. S. Maria Trastevere. Rome _ Ravenna. S. Quentin. Chartres. Rheims (1240, destroyed 1794.) Amiens (1288, destroyed 1825.) _ etc.
Later on, these Labyrinths were used as instruments of penance for non-fulfilment of vows of pilgrimage to the Holy land, & were called 'Chemins de Jerusalem'. The pilgrims followed the windings of the Maze on their knees, & the centre was called 'Le Ciel'. Some of these Labyrinths were destroyed because, "children by noisily tracking out their tortuous paths, occasioned disturbance during divine service'.
We have no ancient example of an ecclesiastical Labyrinth in any English church, but our turf cut mazes are undoubtedly of mediæval, ecclesiastical origin _ They are all situated near a church or a monastic settlement, and still remain at Breamore

Alkborough. Wing. Rutlandshire. Boughton Green, Northants. Saffron Walden. Sneinton, Notts. & St Catherine's Hill, Chilcombe. etc.

The priory of St Michael's, Breamore, was founded for Austin Canons about 1129. & the Miz-maze may be connected with the priory. In Elizabethan times these English mazes would seem to have been secularised _ Titania thus bears witness —

" The nine-men's-morris is filled up with mud ;

And the quaint mazes in the wanton green,

For lack of tread, are undistinguishable = "

They were locally called "Julian Bowers". Troy Towns (Troi in Welsh means to turn) "Shepherd's races" & "Miz-mazes" —
The renaissance garden mazes, in which the paths were misleading have no relation to the Labyrinth type in which the paths always lead continuously to the centre _(c.f. Lethaby. Architecture. Mysticism & Myth.)

Antiquaries seem to be agreed that Bokerly ditch was a defensive
boundary, but there has been much disagreement as to its makers.
Celtic? Belgic? Pre-Roman? were the received opinions before Genᵗˡ
Pitt Rivers conducted a series of excavations through the rampart &
ditch of Bokerly near the present high road from Sarum to Blandford.
Roman coins, & New Forest pottery ware of Romano British patterns, were
found in the body of the rampart — where they could not have got except at the time when it was first made — "It was evident that
a settlement must have existed on the ground before the dyke was thrown
up, the greater part of the coins & relics were found in the lowest
part of the rampart, in dark mould, just over the old surface line".
The conclusion arrived at from the evidence of Genᵗˡ Pitt Rivers' exca-

Bokerly Ditch, crossing Martin Down — from Blagdon Hill —

vations was that this rampart was thrown up by Romanised Britons as a defence against the Saxons . "It was a defensive position taken up on the Roman Road for the defence of the country to the westward" – "Bokerly dyke appears to have run from the high hilly ground in Martin wood on the right, which was originally continuous with the Forest of Holt, across the open valley to the Forest of Cranborne Chase on the left, & to have been intended to defend the open & accessible country between these two Forest districts ." "the crookedness of Bokerly dyke arose from the constructors availing themselves of the hollows, as they occurred in the ground, to dig their ditch, throwing up the earth on the higher ground, by conforming to the

Bokerly ditch
near Woodyates
looking towards
Rockbourne Knoll.
Hale purlieu in the
far distance ✤

inequalities of surface in this way. They obtained the relief they de-
-sired with less expenditure of labour, but the general direction was
determined by considerations of defence, that can clearly be recognised:
'Blagdon Hill is the highest part of the line of Bokerly Dyke & might
perhaps be called the key of the position'-
Admirable models of these excavations are to be seen at the Farnham Museum.
The rampart is now between 30 & 40 feet high on the North side, 12
feet high on the South side, & when new, must have been higher, &
it was probably surmounted by a wattle stockade. The
ditch was much deeper than it is now - When the excavations were
made, 6 feet of siltings were found to have accumulated on the
bottom of Bokerly ditch.

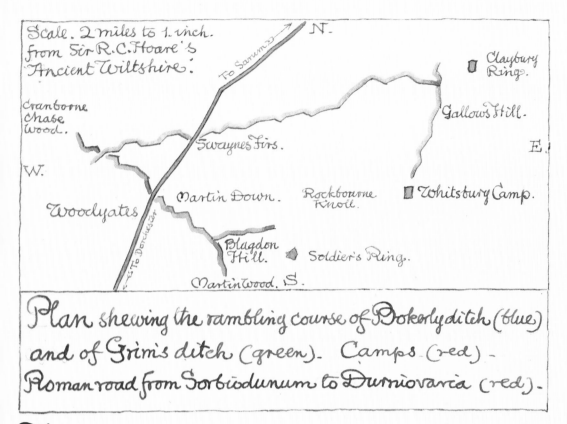

Scale. 2 miles to 1 inch.
from Sir R. C. Hoare's
'Ancient Wiltshire'.

N.

To Sarum

Claybury
Ring.

Cranborne
Chase
Wood.

Gallows Hill.

W.

Swaynes Firs.

E.

Woodyates

Martin Down.

Rockbourne
Knoll.

Whitsbury Camp.

To Dorchester

Blagdon
Hill.

Soldier's Ring.

MartinWood. S.

Plan shewing the rambling course of Bokerly ditch (blue) and of Grim's ditch (green). Camps (red). Roman road from Sorbiodunum to Durniovaria (red).

The above plan shews the relative positions of the two ancient boundary ditches of Cranborne Chase. Grim's ditch is broad & shallow, with banks on either side of about the same heigth, used here & there as a cartway, & having no defensive appearance. It suggests a tribal boundary. The opposition to an enemy coming from the North (which is asserted by the great rampart of Bokerly ditch,) is nowhere suggested by the low banks of Grims ditch. But I can readily understand (with some experience of cattle-straying from our common) that these banks when surmounted with a wattle would be a sufficient tribal barrier, where the wandering herds of prehistoric men might meet, but would not mingle.

The Roman Road from Sarum to Badbury Rings. Looking South. Shewing the present highroad on part of its course.

The Roman occupation of Britannia wrought many changes in our landscape, which remain despite the chances of 1500 years. To our trees they added the elm, plane, lime, walnut, sweet chestnut See Note p. 164 poplar, & most of our fruit trees — They made camps & earthworks with far sighted purpose, & specially the Romans introduced a large planned grasp of design that was wholly wanting in the Brythonic mind. A British hill track-way is known by its wandering course. A British camp follows the contour of the hill. A British village shews a rambling plan, & straight lines & rectilinear forms, would seem to have been alien to the earlier race. When I say — introduced — I do not mean to suggest that any of the great Roman qualities of design were assimilated by the Romano-British. These qualities were destined to lie dormant for centuries after the evacuation of Britannia. But the type of our present comprehensive means of communication still remains as a great landmark across the downs of Cranborne Chase. Codrington (Roman Roads in Britain) thus describes it "The present road then turns towards the West, & the Roman road, here called Ackling Dyke, goes straight on, & is very perfect for 4 miles across the downs. It is 5 yards wide across the top, & 4. 5. or 6 feet or more high. The gravel top has been dug away in places to a depth of 2 or 3 feet for the sake of the material. Traces of the side ditches remain, & in several places they cut the bank & ditch surrounding a barrow. This is perhaps the most striking example of the embankment of a Roman road remaining in the country. It runs for miles in a straight line in bold & sharp relief over the open down, & the magnitude of the work & its"

The Roman Road from Badbury Rings to Sarum. Looking North. shewing the bank cut by the cross road from Cranborne to Standley

situation are alike imposing". The roadway on the top of this embankment was made of gravel, which must have come from an old sea-beach 4 miles to the S.E, in the Reading beds. This top coating was about 3 feet thick, & rested on a base of rammed chalk.* "The destruction of the Roman roads for the sake of their materials, (where stone was available they were paved) began long ago, as Camden & others testify, but their wholesale obliteration took place when turnpike roads were constructed along them or near them, in the latter part of the 18th, & the beginning of the 19th century. It would appear that the more usual plan was to use the materials of the old embankment to make a wider road, the height being reduced to insignificance in the process, & in time still further reduced by wear. Thus, the Salisbury & Blandford road, where it takes the line of the Roman road near Woodyates, is not sensibly raised above the surface of the ground, while beyond, in both directions, where it has not been destroyed for the sake of the materials, the narrower embankment of the Roman road remains 5 or 6 feet high." (Codrington) — This is the part of the road shewn on page 162.

Note. The Institutes of Justinian decreed that roadways through holdings should be 8 ft wide in the straight & 16 feet where the road turned. (J. W. Shore.)

* Section of the Salisbury & Dorchester Roman Road. Genl Pitt Rivers. vol III p. 74

Surface mould - 5 inches. Gravel with rounded pebbles - 6 inches - rammed chalk rubble - 6 inches. Gravel as before - 10 inches - rammed chalk rubble. 6 inches.

Note. Loudon. Arboretum et Fruticetum, gives this list of aboriginal trees, etc, oak, Birch, Alder, Scots pine. Mountain Ash. Juniper. Elder. Holly, Dog rose. Sweetgale, Heath, Ivy, Mistle-toe. Butcher's broom, Spurge laurel. Beech(?) Yew(?) Furzel?) Box (?) Wych elm. Spindle, privet. For full list see vol. I. p. 27

Barrows on Handley Hill.

* a single layer of nodular flints laying on the old surface line _ The total height from the old surface line to the top of the road was 3 feet.

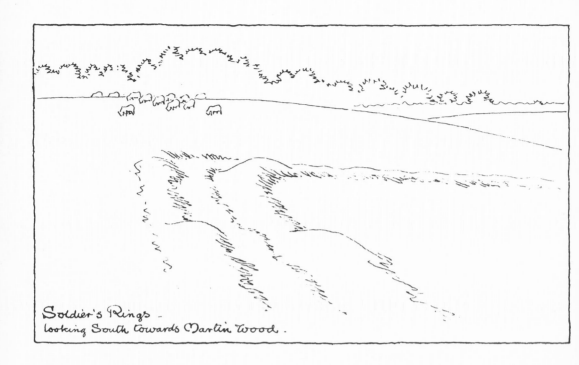

Soldier's Rings -
looking South towards Martin Wood .

Soldier's Rings are Roman earth-works constructed
for a purpose at present unknown — Excavation might ex-
-plain their use — They are situated in a fold of the downs
between Damerham & Martin , & do not suggest a
military position — The precise execution of these low-banks
& shallow ditches is very remarkable, & contrasts with
the rambling lines of the British villages, & with the huge
dykes of the Romano British & West Saxons.
Sir Richard Colt Hoare thus describes Soldier's Rings —
— "Recrossing the vale a little more to the Eastward, I
found a most curious Earthen-work, on the declivity of a vale
of rich turf leading to Damerham . It is known by the vulgar
name of Soldier's Rings — This work is very novel & singular
both in form & construction, & unlike any earthen work we

have yet found – Its form presents an irregular pentangle: the Western side is straight, & the Eastern terminates in a point. . . . The inside of the area contains 27½ acres, & the circumference of the work is 1540 yards, the greatest depth of the vallum is 8 feet. The construction of the ag- -ger differs from any I have seen, & from its weakness cannot have been raised for the purposes of defence: it is finished with a more than usual degree of regularity & presents a section of one low rampart between two of a greater heigth : this work occupies the declivity of a hill at the head of two slight vallies." (Ancient Wiltshire – South – p. 234.)

Looking North towards Damerham knoll.

Note to p.34. <u>Deer on the Common</u>. On Jan 20. 1908. Humphrey & I had a memorable deer-drive on Ibsley Common. It happened thus — We were walking home from Greenford, after a morning spent in watching the deer-hounds vainly hunting does round & round Roe, & Milkham, & Redshoot, & Pinnick. We came through Appleslade, as there I thought we should see some of the disturbed deer. So we did. & 4 does preceded us through the wood. Then, as we crossed the plain, we spied a buck, near Paddy Bussy's Firs : he leisurely made off, over the brow of the hill, & we hurriedly followed, to be rewarded by the sight of 5 bucks, all at gaze, on a little hill rising out of Roden's bottom. They regarded our advent with complete unconcern, & only moved over the little hill, towards the road, after they had completely satisfied their curiosity. Humphrey then went to the left, & I to the right — both unseen now by the deer — & stalked them with the intention of driving them off Rockford on to Ibsley Common : in which purpose we were successful, as when we emerged to view, they took their only open road, & stotted off across the heather & sweetgale for Digden bottom, crossed the Docken's water rather reluctantly, & then paused in the bog, & again stood at gaze. Humphrey then made for Newlands bridge, while the deer & I mutually watched each other, after a time they picked their way across the bog & went up the hill, towards Newlands, but here they were headed by Humphrey, & were joined by 3 does which he had put up in the heather. The little herd of 8 deer now cantered across Whitefield plain, to the great surprise of the ponies, one of which reared violently & waved his shackled forelegs at the intruders — But the deer took no notice & trotted on to the top end of little Chibden bottom. Here they stopped — Now our project was to shepherd them into Great Chibden bottom, & shew an unwonted sight to the inhabitants of Cuckoo Hill; but this was too much ; The old bucks seemed to think they had been playing long enough with us ; & the herd trotted steadily off across the plain to Ledenhall, despite our desperate efforts to head them — So ended an afternoon of beau- tiful sights —

On the following day, Humphrey & Doris put up 5 does in the Furze at Ledenhall

On Feby 17. 1909. I saw 4 bucks & 3 does at Leaden hall.

In April 1909. Humphrey saw 2 bucks & 3 does at Leaden hall.

# Post Scriptum

I like a book either to have a preface or a postscript. In fact, I like both a greeting & a farewell from the author. I like to know why he sought his own particular subject, & in what mood he completed the long work of patient days. I like to compare my estimate of his results with his intention. Accordingly, I suppose a similar vein of quiet curiosity in you, my reader, as you come to the end of these leisurely pages. Curiosity — that a man should spend laborious days with pen & pencil, writing & drawing the chronicle of an obscure locality, at a time when most men cared for eager competition in a hundred different spheres, & when England was humming with a hundred different party cries — Well, man does not live by competition alone, nor by party meetings. A remnant is left of those who do not willingly compete; who love golden silence, rather than silver speech-making; & who think that work rightly done is the first thing needful in these days of chatter. I love dealing with materials so as to express a designed plan. I love mother Earth. I like endeavour & excellence

that come by the way, that grow out of every-day life,
— not forced by Exhibitions, & Success, & Fuss: and the
change & chance of Time that have brought us here,
have likewise provided my subject, & my equipment for
making this book.    I think that all good country
books are rooted in a locality — They may almost
seem to be dormant in the soil, awaiting the beneficent
advent that gives them shape: and if there is any good
in these pages, it is born of my love of Earth, and of
re-creation. I have wished to record my keen enjoyment in
the life around us, & I think that happiness grows from
quiet, curious interest in the affairs & setting of our own
daily life. Thus we may gain contentment, & knowledge
founded on questioning observation, & thus we may hand on
some vision of the days that pass & are no more — if we
see & record with understanding — If — ah, there's
the rub — M^r Oldbuck hated 'But' — Most of us
dread 'If' — And I also fear it; however, you
know my intention; it is for you to estimate; and so,
Fare-well — May the nether pavement of good
intentions not be increased by The Book of
Gorley —

Finis

Appendix — In 1908. There was no rain from July 18 to Aug.ᵗ 19. During the drought, the cooped hens at Doyle's Court were raided by some animal. Eventually, one of the night-watch keepers, shot a badger in the act of killing a hen — Badgers usually eat roots, frogs, earth-nuts, beetles etc, & so when Gates, the under-keeper, told me of this, I expressed surprise to which he replied — "When the ground's hard, you may depend upon't, badgers is gifted for hens" —

The poisonous effects of yew — "My only personal experience is that a horse of mine died after feeding on lawn-mowings which chiefly consisted of dry, fallen yew-leaves. It is generally supposed that yew is much more poisonous when wilted i.e dried". Champion Russell. "From the experiments of Professor Wiborg, it appears that yew-leaves, eaten alone, are fatal to animals, particularly to horses; but that when mixed with twice or thrice as much oats, they may be used without danger. This neutralisation of the poisonous qualities of the yew by another vegetable may explain, to a certain degree, the diversity of opinion upon their effects; it being possible that some animals, which have eaten of the yew without inconvenience, had shortly before eaten heartily of some other vegetable". Loudon. Vol IV. p.2089 —90.

Stephen Shutler says that dog foxes bark — bow — wow — wow. vixens — bow — wow —

On the South side of Ibsley bridge is the following inscription. "This Bridge built for the County by    172. J. Watkins of Ringwood stonemason 1797"

Rainfall at Cuckoo Hill.

| Month | 1905 | 1906 | 1907 | 1908 | 1909 | 1910 | 1911 |
|---|---|---|---|---|---|---|---|
| January | | 7.38 | .80 | 1.47 | 1.07 | 3.81 | 1.25 |
| February | | 3.20 | 1.41 | 1.52 | .42 | 4.13 | 2.08 |
| March | | 2.17 | .57 | 3.70 | 4.24 | .93 | 2.25 |
| April | | 1.07 | 4.13 | 2.54 | 1.41 | 2.37 | 1.67 |
| May | | 2.12 | 2.10 | 2.34 | 1.87 | 1.81 | 1.35 |
| June | | 1.29 | 1.61 | .56 | 2.61 | 3.63 | 2.51 |
| July | | 1.61 | 1.19 | 1.99 | 3.36 | 2.14 | .32 |
| August | | 1.06 | 2.05 | 5.20 | 2.71 | 2.36 | 1.32 |
| September | 1.53 | .87 | .63 | 1.78 | 3.79 | .22 | 1.16 |
| October | 1.34 | 6.83 | 8.86 | 1.78 | 8.64 | 4.70 | 3.15 |
| November | 5.24 | 4.76 | 3.14 | 1.19 | .61 | 3.93 | 4.28 |
| December | -.82 | 2.09 | 4.92 | 3.97 | 4.37 | 6.19 | 9.77 |
| Total (Inches) | | 34.45 | 31.41 | 28.04 | 35.10 | 36.22 | 31.11 |

Remarks ___ The heaviest rainfall in 24 hours in 1906 was on Jan 2. 1 inch .42 - rain measureable on 136 days.

The heaviest rainfall in 24 hours in 1907 was on Aug 17. 1 inch - 10 rain days 160

------------------------- 1908 ..... Aug 28. 1 inch .12 ..... 173

In 1908 we had 2 heavy snowfalls April 24 & 25. (20 & .63) Dec 28 & 29 (25 & 36)
The heaviest rainfall in 24 hours in 1909 was on Sept 28. 2.25 inches
There was another heavy rainfall on Oct 26. 2.01 inches. rain
fell on 162 days during 1909. The heaviest rainfall in 24 hours
in 1910 was on Oct 12. 1.40 inch. rain fell on 193 days.
In 1911. heavy rain fell Nov 11. 1.20 & Dec 6 .1.03. In July
rain (.32) fell on only one day. During the year, on 160 days.

173.

Appendix — William Tame loqr. 'One of the Crown tenants, he got behind wi' his rent, but kep' on coming to the audit dinner jist the same. Well, the Crown they talk it over, & then they says as how he owed 'em a lot of money & mussen do it agen, & so they'd let en off, but till he paid his rent reglar he mussen come to the audit dinner. So he said, 'Thankee'; but he told me, that he'd rather owe the money & have the dinner'.

'That minds me o' the man who allers put his chair par-ticlar at dinner, & then used to eat hisself up to the table; then he knowed that he'd a finished his dinner. But one day they bested en; for they shifted his chair; & bumby he found that he didden get no nearer, tho' he kep' on eating — so he never know'd when he'd finished.

Lord Nelson, the present owner of Trafalgar, is the venerable advocate of free & open churches. Year's ago, his uncle was domestic chaplain of the little chapel of Standlinch, just below Trafalgar, which was wont to be filled with Nelson retainers. One Sunday evening, wonderful to relate, a stranger appeared in the chapel. The chaplain — astonished at the intrusion — stopped the service. 'Where d'ee come from?' he said. 'Downton, good now', replied the stranger, whereat the chaplain sd., 'Well, don't let me ever see yr. face here again'. (Elias Squarey) 1907

Appendix — Current wage for unskilled labour – 2$^s$. 6$^d$ a day – for skilled labour – 3$^s$ a day. Cutting & tieing oats. 11$^s$ an acre. Mowing meadow grass 6/ an acre. A load of manure – 3/, in place – A man, cart, & horse at work for the day. 6/- Drawing a load of chalk from Whitsbury (1½ ton) & spreading. 6/- the load costs 1/6 A fathom of 'More' wood. (More. Moore — a root c, f. Chaucer. glossary, Barnes' glossary, Webster;) 6/. A fathom is 5 feet long. 5 feet high, & 2½ feet wide — 3 fathoms equal 2 cords —
A cord of wood. From 7./ to 10/. A cord is 8 feet long. 4 feet high, & 4 feet wide. (a cord makes a cart-load) Cutting 100 faggots of furze on the common — 3/6 –
. . . . . . . . . . . . . turves. 6$^d$ a hundred. — a thousand, cut in a day
Hedging. 6$^d$ or 5$^d$ a lug – i, e, 16½ feet – a lug stick is used for taking down smoked bacon in open chimnies, & being handy, & tolerably uniform in length I suppose it became accepted as a measure.
Threshing oats per sack – 10$^d$ a sack.
Cider-making 6$^d$ – 8$^d$ a gallon, according to the price of apples 1$^d$ a gallon. For making, if you supply the apples & additional labour required. Thomas has charged this modest price for making ever since he started his cider press, 37 years ago.
Note. Cider thus made, should be drunk within a year, or it will get 'hard'. If you want it to keep longer, you must add some sugar — thus – draw off some cider dissolve your sugar in this, pour it back through the bung-hole, & re-cork.

Chalking our land here makes it work better, overcomes club-root in cabbages etc., weakens weeds such as sorrel, poor Jack, & 'Bolden' (corn chrysanthemum), & the benefit lasts for many years. It is best to do it in the autumn, then the winter frosts disintegrate the chalk which is ploughed in, in the spring. Whitsbury chalk, which is soapy & friable is much better for the purpose than Cranborne chalk wh is hard. For use in building, the local plan was to spread block chalk in the spring, & such blocks as did not break up with a year's weathering were considered to be fit to be used, while the dis-integrated blocks benefitted the land. Chalking, or marling, dates back to Romano-British times. (J. W. Shore.) See. Folk-Memory. Johnson - P. 203 on ancient chalking -

* Note p 59. This entry suggests a wet night in more senses than one. The custom was to brew a small cask of beer for each quarter-night meeting - If the night happened to be very rough, the attendance might be scanty — but the cask, tho' small for a full meeting, would be large for an empty meeting, & the few who came used to feel that the occasion demanded an effort, accordingly, they did their best to finish the small cask — result — beating out candles — horse-play — fine - 2ˢ. 6ᵈ

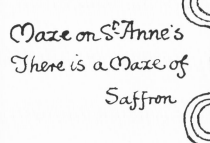

Maze on St Anne's Hill near Nottingham.
There is a Maze of a similar design at
Saffron Walden.

Maze at Pimperne near Blandford
which was ploughed up in the year 1730
This design is unique.

Maze on St Catherine's hill
Chilcombe nr Winchester.

177.

Monument to Sir John Constable
in St Martins church Ibsley
Scale - ¾ inch to one foot -

179.